Alternate Reality Games

Using textual analysis, interviews with game designers, audience surveys, and close analysis of player forum discussion, this book examines the unique nature of the producer/consumer relationship within promotional alternate reality games (ARGs).

Historically, ARGs are rooted in advertising as much as they are in narrative storytelling. As designers often have to respond to player actions as the game progresses, players can have an impact on the storyline, on character behaviour, and potentially on the final resolution of the narrative. This book explores how both media consumers and producers are responding to this new reconfiguration of the producer/consumer/prosumer dynamic in order to better understand the diverse advertising experiences available to media audiences today.

With a focus on participatory culture and the political economy of promotional communications, this in-depth analysis of ARGs will appeal to academics and researchers in the fields of games, film, advertising, and media and cultural studies.

Stephanie Janes is a British Academy Postdoctoral Research Fellow at King's College, London. She has previously lectured in Media & Communications at the University of East London, and Media Arts at Royal Holloway, University of London, where she also completed her PhD. Her research interests are in film and media promotion, and media convergence with an emphasis on film and gaming. She has previously published on promotional ARGs for films in *Arts and the Market* and edited collections including *The Politics of Ephemeral Digital Media: Permanence and Obsolescence in Paratexts*, eds. Sara Pesce and Paolo Noto, and *Alternate Reality Games and the Cusp of Digital Gameplay*, eds. Antero Garcia and Greg Niemeyer.

Routledge Critical Advertising Studies
Series Editor: Jonathan Hardy

Routledge Critical Advertising Studies tracks the profound changes that have taken place in the field of advertising. Presenting thought-provoking scholarship from both prominent scholars and emerging researchers, these ground-breaking short form publications cover cutting-edge research concerns and contemporary issues within the field. Titles in the series explore emerging trends, present detailed case studies and offer new assessments of topics such as branded content, economic surveillance, product placement, gender in marketing, and promotional screen media. Responding quickly to the latest developments in the field, the series is intellectually compelling, refreshingly open, provocative and action-oriented.

Alternative Reality Games
Stephanie Janes

For more information about this series, please visit: https://www.routledge. com/Routledge-Critical-Advertising-Studies/book-series/RCAS

Alternate Reality Games
Promotion and Participatory Culture

Stephanie Janes

Routledge
Taylor & Francis Group

LONDON AND NEW YORK

First published 2020 by Routledge

2 Park Square, Milton Park, Abingdon, Oxon OX14 4RN

605 Third Avenue, New York, NY 10017

Routledge is an imprint of the Taylor & Francis Group, an informa business

First issued in paperback 2022

British Library Cataloguing-in-Publication Data
A catalogue record for this book is available from the British Library

Library of Congress Cataloging-in-Publication Data
A catalog record for this book has been requested

ISBN: 978-0-815-38680-3 (hbk)
ISBN: 978-1-03-233812-5 (pbk)
DOI: 10.4324/9781351174749

Typeset in Times New Roman
by Apex CoVantage LLC

For my husband, who now knows more than he ever wanted to know about alternate reality games.

Contents

Illustrations

Figures

Tables

Acknowledgements

This book is based on PhD research that would not have been possible without generous scholarships provided by the Department of Media Arts, Royal Holloway, University of London, for which I am extremely grateful. The guidance of my doctoral supervisor, Prof. Barry Langford, and the support of the whole department were invaluable and greatly appreciated. My series editor, Prof. Jonathan Hardy, has also been incredibly generous with his time and feedback as the thesis made its long and winding journey to book format.

The project could not have been completed without the assistance of interviewees and survey respondents who took the time to talk to me about their experiences of ARGs. I would therefore like to express my immense gratitude to Adrian Hon, John Christiano, and Sean Stewart, who took a genuine interest in the project and provided me with supportive and informative feedback throughout.

Introduction

It's 7 May 2010. You've been waiting for info on the new J.J. Abrams film for months and it's finally here! You load up the *Super 8* (2011) teaser trailer on YouTube and settle in with anticipation. It's dramatic, but it's not giving much away. In a small town in 1970s Ohio, a train carrying top secret cargo from Area 51 collides head-on with a truck, careering towards it on the tracks. Huge explosions ensue – there can't possibly be any survivors. But as the dust settles on the wreckage, something rumbles – a creature is fighting its way out of the metal shipping container. As it finally punches through the reinforced steel doors, we cut to a shattered camera lens. A film reel flickers rapidly through. You can see letters written on it, but it's moving too fast to make them out.

Almost.

You pause the video and skim back to the start of the reel, moving frame by frame to see the letters spell out a phrase:

Scariest Thing I Ever Saw

This is creepy. But you've seen this before. The trailer for *Cloverfield* (Matt Reeves 2008) didn't even have the film's title in it. It contained only the release date and home video footage of a leaving party in New York being interrupted by an attack on the city. The release date turned out to be a website and the beginning of a conspiracy theory-filled alternate reality game. This is J.J.'s calling card. So you open a web browser and hazard a guess at:

Scariestthingieversaw.com

Sure enough, a website appears looking remarkably like a remote PC desktop from 1992. Suddenly a prompt appears to 'print all documents'. Almost without thinking you hit OK. Your wireless printer springs into life and spits out a single line of text at the top of the page stating:

'stop posting publicly. I can answer your questions, I have proof'[1]

Now this is REALLY creepy. Too creepy to deal with on your own. But you've fallen headfirst down the rabbit hole and there's no going back. So you head to Unfiction.com and join the Super 8 ARG forum where the collective detective is already furiously deciphering who sent the message, why they sent it, and where it will lead to next. Welcome to the world of alternate reality gaming.

***

It is difficult to explain ARGs to newcomers without recounting an experience like the one above. They are complex, collaborative, and deeply involving experiences – genuinely unique forms of storytelling and notoriously difficult to define. ARGs are often mistaken for console games that tie in with films, like *Enter the Matrix* (Atari Inc. 2005), virtual worlds like *Second Life* (Linden Lab 2003), or massively multiplayer online roleplaying games (MMORPGS) like *World of Warcraft* (Blizzard Entertainment 2004). In more recent discussions, 'alternate reality' conjures visions of virtual or augmented reality technologies, with users plugged into a story universe via headsets or smartphones as with *Pokémon GO* (Niantic 2016) or *Jurassic World Alive* (Ludia 2018). They are none of these things but sit instead at a tangled intersection of storytelling and game-playing. Broadly speaking, ARGs are immersive, interactive narratives told across multiple platforms. Game designer Andrea Phillips provides a more thorough definition:

> A cohesive narrative revealed through a series of websites, emails, phone calls, IM [instant messenger], live and in-person events. Players often earn new information to further the plot by cracking puzzles . . . [they] typically organise themselves into communities to share information and speculate on what it all means and where it's all going.
>
> (Phillips 2005)

ARG player forum Unfiction offers a similar definition, echoing the unified perspectives of players and designers:

> A cross-media genre of interactive fiction using multiple delivery and communications media, including television, radio, newspapers, internet, email, SMS, telephone, voicemail, and postal service. Gaming is typically comprised of a secret group of Puppetmasters [PMs] who

author, manipulate, and otherwise control the storyline, related scenarios, and puzzles and a public group of players, the collective detective that attempts to solve the puzzles and thereby win the furtherance of the story.

(*Unfiction* 2011)

ARGs come in varying shapes and sizes with different production contexts and target audiences (Askwith 2006). Film fans produced games extending the narratives of *The Matrix* (Wachowski Siblings 1999) (Metacortechs)[2] and *Minority Report* (Steven Spielberg 2002) (Exocog)[3], immersing players further into existing worlds that they continued to build together. Commercial and monetised models included a monthly subscription format for EA's *Majestic* (2000).[4] This ultimately proved unattractive to players (Pham 2001), but *Perplex City*, built around the purchase of collectible playing cards, was successful for independent UK developer Mind Candy.[5]

However, those formats are less well known than promotional ARGs. These tend to be larger in scale, enabled by substantial marketing budgets from large corporations. The games are rarely produced in-house and are usually contracted out to specialist marketing companies like 42 Entertainment.[6] This is exemplified in Audi's Art of the Heist (Campfire/McKinney+Silver 2005) and Microsoft's ilovebees (42 Entertainment 2004) for Xbox game *Halo 2* (Microsoft Studios 2004). This also overlaps with what Ivan Askwith (2006) terms the 'narrative extension' ARG, which is attached to another media property. For example, the Lost Experience ARG served to fill the summer hiatus between seasons 2 and 3 of TV series *Lost* (ABC 2004–2010). It therefore had a more explicit remit to extend the show's narrative as well as promote the series overall. Many games fit multiple categories, further complicating a concise definition of ARGs.

The genre's history is firmly rooted in advertising. The first fully fledged ARG was The Beast – a promotional game for Steven Spielberg's *A.I.: Artificial Intelligence* (2001) launched by a team at Microsoft. Yet academic research is reluctant to engage with them on these terms. Askwith identifies a key difficulty when he describes ARGs as a 'collision of traditional promotional marketing and new immersive narrative content' (2006: 16). The two are often viewed as incompatible, and scholarship tends to focus on creative content over the commercial intent of ARGs, arguing for the games as something 'more' than 'just' marketing. Several studies focus on their potential to 'do good' within educational contexts (Piatt 2009; Sheldon 2011; Chess & Booth 2014), social science research (Gordon 2015), or 'serious games' aimed at real-world problem solving (Dondlinger & Mcleod 2015; Hunter 2015).

Rarely are ARGs confronted as pieces of advertising for other media products, despite this being their formative arena. Örnebring's (2007) article is an exception, arguing that ARGs are primarily commercial in nature, and comparing official and fan-made ARGs for the TV series *Alias* (ABC 2001–2006). He concludes that both fan-produced and official ARGs conform to 'corporate goals of marketing and brand building as well as fan audience's goals of pleasurable interaction with fictional worlds' (2007: 445). Even fan-produced games conform to producers' basic intentions, because the power to set limits on these narratives remains within the cultural industries. Their primary purpose is not to invite interaction or participation but to 'create an enjoyable experience that will build the franchise in the minds of the audience' (2007: 50). Örnebring argues this is as easily provided by 'largely redundant' ancillary texts as by offering opportunities for participation (2007: 455).

In contrast, Gray's work (2010) discusses how ARGs function as meaningful paratexts, rather than 'redundant' pieces of marketing. He argues pointedly that building a franchise in the minds of an audience might well require the opportunity for 'interaction, networking and audience participation in mediated narratives'. A text's commercial prerogative does not necessarily 'obviate its substance' (Gray 2010: 209). This is a positive attempt to highlight the meaning-making potential of such paratexts, but nonetheless shifts the spotlight away from their promotional intent and onto their creative content.

In less text-focussed analyses, ARGs are considered as sites for participatory culture and consumer empowerment (Jenkins 2006; McGonigal 2008). Jenkins discusses them in terms of affective economics and brand awareness but emphasises that 'for the most hard-core players, these games can be so much more' (2006: 130). He recognises their commercial intent but prefers to view them in the context of the empowering nature of convergence culture and collective intelligence. Quoting game designer and scholar Jane McGonigal, he argues ARGs can affect the way people think and behave in their everyday lives (Jenkins 2006: 130–131). McGonigal herself has written extensively on ARGs in terms of performativity and play.[7] Again, rather than discussing them as promotional devices, she is more concerned with how collaborative play prompts players to attempt real-world problem solving, and the implications of such collective intelligence for aspects of social life.

Askwith's white paper (2007) is aimed at marketers considering using promotional games in their strategy. He observes that ARGs can engage consumers with a product before it becomes available, construct brand awareness, and are cost-effective compared to traditional campaigns. However, they do not necessarily generate quick purchase decisions and can appear complicated, inaccessible, or appealing only to a small, committed audience demographic. The key to overcoming this is to understand that ARGs attract all kinds of players, some of whom have as much fun watching others play as participating themselves (Askwith 2007: 23–24). Askwith therefore suggests producers should view ARGs as materials which must perform more than the basic advertising function but, almost paradoxically, must not announce themselves as advertising. This requires media companies to shift their mindset, and Askwith suggests mainstream media industries may struggle to see the value of a dedicated, smaller audience over the more quantifiable value of a casual, mass audience (2007: 20). The use of such strategies can be considered an acknowledgement of the growing importance of that dedicated audience, and an increasing focus on building brand loyalty over immediately visible returns on investment. Unfortunately, the difficulties in defining ARGs make it difficult to pinpoint their value to marketers. ARGs straddle categories of existing industry strategies and theories which are themselves often conflated, including relationship marketing, viral marketing, immersive marketing, pervasive gaming, and affective economics. ARGs enter into discourses around the 'gamification' of marketing and arguably work towards constructing brand communities. Their tendency to mask or deny their status as pieces of marketing also resonates with contemporary debates around branded content (Goodman 2006; Hardy 2017a, 2017b).[8]

There is no disputing the commercial purpose of promotional ARGs. What seems to be debatable is their relative value as mechanisms for social change, creative storytelling, or marketing tools. They can, of course, perform all these functions – but one is always deemed of higher value than another in competing discourses. This book addresses this by providing a more holistic approach to examining the form, history, and function of promotional ARGs in contemporary media marketing. It considers both production and reception contexts and uses this analysis to challenge received notions about participatory culture, consumer/producer relationships, and political economies of labour in digital promotional culture. It also focusses primarily on promotional ARGs for films, as ARGs for TV shows or consumer products serve different purposes and engage with narrative storytelling in different ways which make them difficult to compare effectively, for example, TV ARGs often need to maintain viewer interest in existing storylines during a summer hiatus. ARGs for cars, meanwhile, must work within brand value guidelines but arguably have more space for original storytelling and do not face the same constraints as either TV or film ARGs, which work with existing intellectual property (IP).

The book uses primary research, mostly conducted over a three-year period (2011–2014), involving textual analysis of ARGs, interviews with game producers, a player survey, and netnographic (Kozinets 2010) analysis of player forum discussions. In addition, it consults contemporary research on digital marketing across subject areas ranging from media and cultural studies to marketing, advertising, and business studies. This multimethod, interdisciplinary approach involves specific challenges, particularly in the textual analysis of digital ephemera. A great deal of game content is swiftly removed by rights holders after serving its purpose in the marketing campaign. Most game sites are therefore no longer accessible. The few available via the Internet Archive are often incomplete or, in the case of Flash sites, no longer function.[9] There is therefore some reliance on players' own archiving and remembrance of the games, as well as the researcher's own game experiences and personal archiving of screenshots and so forth.[10] This is a significant problem in analysing and archiving these experiences, previously addressed by researchers in this field (Janes 2016), particularly Kim Walden's (2014, 2016) work on Flynn Lives, the promotional ARG for *Tron: Legacy* (Joseph Kosinski 2010). Even player forums have started to deteriorate. Unfiction.com still exists as a website but the forum is not available, so much of the discussion under examination here is unavailable to re-examine.

This is an issue in advertising research more generally, where work is not routinely archived and/or made accessible to the public or researchers. This is often due to IP restrictions or a general sense that such material is not of value once it has performed its promotional purpose. ARG material is also designed to be experiential – its value is in its exclusivity. It should therefore be noted that links and references in this book are as up to date as possible, but it is likely these will also become less accessible over time. It is not the purpose of this book to comment extensively on these methodological challenges, but it is important to state that the lack of long-term and systematic archiving of these sorts of ephemera means it will become increasingly difficult to study them in the future.

In terms of the book's structure, Chapter 1 offers a broad outline of ARG structures and rules. It then provides an overview of their emergence in the context of changing media consumption practices, promotional cultures, and marketing practices. Three case studies are introduced in their recent historical and industrial contexts: The Beast was the first example of a fully fledged ARG as well as the first promotional ARG. Many generic traits can therefore be said to have formed during this game. WhySoSerious was developed by prominent producers 42 Entertainment[11] to promote *The Dark Knight* (Christopher Nolan 2008). This was considered a landmark ARG and is a strong example of a game promoting an instalment of an established franchise with a large, pre-existing fanbase. Finally, Super 8 was included as a recent promotional ARG for a film at the time of writing, in which the researcher participated from launch to conclusion. It is also a useful example of a game produced for a J.J. Abrams property. ARGs for previous Abrams projects like *Alias*, *Lost*, and *Cloverfield* meant *Super 8* (2011) came with expectations for an ARG or an innovative marketing campaign. Abrams had become so closely associated with the genre that it was important to include one of these games in a representative selection of promotional film ARGs from the past ten years. Finally, the chapter outlines the rise of the genre in marketing campaigns and possible reasons for its decline.

Chapter 2 extends this discussion to examine how the case studies performed promotional work. It considers each game's relationship to wider campaigns and the films they promoted, questioning their varying degrees of 'connectedness'. It is possible to view ARGs as more/less central to the viewing experience depending on how they are integrated with the film narrative. Finally, it considers how each game employs existing marketing strategies including affective economics, branding/brand communities, and sponsorship.

Chapter 3 unravels one of the key claims of promotional ARGs – the promise of meaningful participation. It outlines current theories of participatory culture and how promotional ARGs challenge the perception of an increasingly informed and empowered media consumer. ARGs arguably make all the promises of co-creation without relinquishing any real power to consumers. This section looks at player perspectives – their expectations and motivations for participating in a promotional ARG, drawing heavily on two bodies of data: the results of a player survey and analysis of forum discussion. This combination provides both self-reported, elicited information and 'in-game' or 'in vivo' expressions of attitudes and opinions, which help to understand player experiences. The survey was aimed predominately at highly active users and performed a signposting function, rather than offering a representative sample. It provided a basis on which to question attitudes expressed by players in vast swathes of forum discussion data.

Unfiction.com was chosen as the location for survey activity as this was a high-profile, active, ARG-specific community, with 33,674 registered members at the time (2014). Forum discussion was collected from three forums to provide data on each case study: Unfiction (UF), Superherohype.com (SHH), and the Cloudmakers Yahoo! Group (CM). The Beast was played primarily via the CM site and Super 8 via UF. WhySoSerious was played in UF but saw more activity on SHH. All forums were legally and easily available to view publicly without becoming a member. However, the UF forums have since shut down, again highlighting the challenges of archiving these experiences. All forum discussion has been anonymised and no users have been identified either by name or forum handle.[12]

Having discussed participation, Chapter 4 addresses the related issue of the role of promotional ARGs in harnessing that participation to provide free digital marketing labour. It considers how the blurred boundaries between reality/fiction and content/advertising problematises concepts of digital labour, where audiences (wittingly or otherwise) perform marketing work for free. It also considers this from a producer perspective, acknowledging the two producer/consumer relationships at play: player/PM and player/media company. Each have their own dynamics and affect each party's perceptions of the labour involved in promotional ARGs.

To inform this discussion, data was collected from in-depth interviews with game designers. Access to media companies proved difficult to acquire, so discussions surrounding their intentions and expectations come predominately from the perspective of their contractors, or interviews with corporate spokespeople in trade or mainstream press. It is important to keep in mind the potential biases and limitations of these sources. They are usually unable to offer precise information, for example, regarding campaign budgets and may need to protect ongoing business interests and relationships with former clients.

Interviews were conducted with Sean Stewart (Lead Writer on The Beast), John Christiano, (CEO of Project C) and Adrian Hon (founder of Six to Start). After their groundbreaking work on The Beast, Stewart joined Jordan Weisman (Creative Director of Microsoft's Entertainment Division) and Elan Lee (Lead Game Designer at Microsoft Games Studios) in forming independent creative content agency 42 Entertainment in 2003. Lee and Stewart left the company in 2007 to form Fourth Wall Studios, before 42 Entertainment embarked on WhySoSerious.

Christiano founded the Texas-based digital agency Project C in 2002. It was involved with *Super 8*'s ARG in 2010, developed and produced by various contractors working for Amblin, Paramount, and Bad Robot. Project C were responsible for some elements of the game, but others were run by marketing agency Watson D/G. This provided a particularly interesting perspective on a project comprised of multiple moving parts developed by different stakeholders.

Hon was a lead moderator on the Cloudmakers Yahoo! discussion board. He went on to work for London-based Mind Candy on the stand-alone ARG *Perplex City*, founding his own company, Six to Start, in 2007.[13] Six to Start have worked on transmedia marketing campaigns for properties including *Spooks Code 9* (David Wolstencroft 2008) for the BBC, *Misfits* (Howard Overman 2009–2013) for Channel 4, and *Young Bond* (Charlie Higson 2008–2014) for Puffin Books. Hon's perspective is valuable in that he can speak from both sides of the curtain, having experienced ARGs as both PM and player.

Interviews were complemented with trade press articles and interviews, for example, *Advertising Age*, *Brand Strategy*, and mainstream titles including *Wired* and *The New York Times*. Transcripts of post-game chat between players and PMs of The Beast offered an insight into the early relationship between players and PMs, and transcripts from panels at ARGFest-o-Con 2007 have also been consulted.[14] All are available online or in print in the public domain. Access to documents from the Cloudmakers' Yahoo! group requires membership of the group; however, membership is not restricted.

This book aims not only to introduce the relatively unknown world of alternate reality gaming to readers who are new to the genre, but also to shine some light on two key issues surrounding their use as promotional materials. The games are frequently heralded as empowering, collaborative, and co-creative, and this is often true to the experience of many players. But, within the context of promotion and marketing, we need a more critical, in-depth discussion about the terms of that collaboration and the power dynamics at play in promotional ARGs which seemingly require audiences to perform marketing labour in return for entertaining experiences. This is far more complex than previous research has allowed for, and this book seeks to unpick those complexities, using research based on the grounded and lived-through experiences of both players and puppetmasters.

Notes

1 http://super8.wikibruce.com/File:STIES-Console100507_Printout.jpg
2 https://metacortex.netninja.com/my_notes/history.html
3 www.miramontes.com/writing/exocog/
4 www.wired.com/2001/05/majestic-invades-your-world/
5 www.perplexcity.com/
6 www.42entertainment.com/
7 For full list of publications, see www.janemcgonigal.com
8 For further reading around branded content, see www.brandedcontentresearch network.org/books-and-articles/
9 https://archive.org/web/
10 Whilst the author has maintained a small archive of screenshots and images for personal use, the use of these images was not permitted by several rights holders and therefore could not be reproduced in this volume. This poses challenges given that this is a heavily visual medium, often best explained in images rather than words. Links to Web Archive copies of sites have been provided wherever possible.
11 www.42entertainment.com
12 All quotations from players (either from forums or survey responses) are italicised throughout this book to differentiate them from other quotations.
13 www.sixtostart.com/

14 The official website describes this conference as 'an annual community organized conference, festival and meet-up designed to offer presentations and events related to alternate reality gaming, transmedia and serious games.' It started as a small meeting in 2003 but developed into a larger conference attracting key industry speakers, and was last held in 2013; http://argfestocon.com/

References

Askwith, I. (2006) *This Is Not (Just) an Advertisement: Understanding Alternate Reality Games*, MIT Convergence Culture Consortium White Paper. Available: http://convergenceculture.org/research/c3_not_just_an_ad.pdf [Accessed 11.01. 2019].

Askwith, I. (2007) *Deconstructing the Lost Experience: In-Depth Analysis of an ARG*, MIT Convergence Culture Consortium White Paper. Available: http://convergenceculture.org/resources/2006/12/deconstructing_the_lost_experi.php [Accessed 11.01.2019].

Chess, S. & Booth, P. (2014) 'Lessons Down a Rabbit Hole: Alternate Reality Gaming in the Classroom', *New Media & Society*, 16(6), pp. 1002–1017.

Cloverfield (2008) dir. Matt Reeves *Tron: Legacy* (2010) dir. Joseph Kosinski.

Dondlinger, M. & Mcleod, J. (2015) 'Solving Real World Problems with Alternate Reality Gaming: Student Experiences in the Global Village Playground Capstone Course Design', *Interdisciplinary Journal of Problem-Based Learning*, 9(2).

Goodman, E. (2006) 'Stealth Marketing and Editorial Integrity', *Texas Law Review*, 85, pp. 83–152.

Gordon, R. (2015) *Alternate Reality Games for Behavioural and Social Science Research*, ETC Press. Available: https://openlibra.com/en/book/alternate-reality-games-for-behavioral-and-social-science-research [Accessed 11.01.2019].

Gray, J. (2010) *Show Sold Separately: Promos, Spoilers, and Other Media Paratexts*, New York, NY: New York University Press.

Hardy, J. (2017a) 'Commentary: Branded Content and Media-Marketing Convergence', *The Political Economy of Communication*, 5(1), pp. 81–87.

Hardy, J. (2017b) 'Sponsored Content Is Compromising Media Integrity', *openDemocracy*, 12.04.2017. Available: www.opendemocracy.net/jonathan-hardy/sponsored-content-is-blurring-line-between-advertising-and-editorial [Accessed 17. 01.2019].

Hunter, L. B. (2015) 'This Is Not a Threat: Conspiracy for Good', *International Journal of Performance Arts and Digital Media*, 11(2), pp. 185–201.

Janes, S. (2016) ' "You Had to Be There" – ARGs and Multiple Durational Temporalities', in Sara Pesce & Paolo Noto, eds., *The Politics of Ephemeral Digital Media*, London: Routledge, pp. 183–197.

Jenkins, H. (2006) *Convergence Culture: Where Old and New Media Collide*, New York, NY; London: New York University Press.

Kozinets, R. (2010) *Netnography: Doing Ethnographic Research Online*, London: Sage.

McGonigal, J. (2008) 'Why I Love Bees: A Case Study in Collective Intelligence Gaming', in K. Salen, ed., *The Ecology of Games*, Cambridge, MA.; London: MIT Press, pp. 199–227.

Örnebring, H. (2007) 'Alternate Reality Gaming and Convergence Culture', *International Journal of Cultural Studies*, 10(4), pp. 445–462.

Pham, A. (2001) 'Game Lacks "Majestic" Interest', *The LA Times*, 26.11.2001. Available: https://web.archive.org/web/20150609050609/http://articles.latimes.com/2001/sep/26/business/fi-49897 [Accessed 11.01.2019].

Phillips, A. (2005) 'Soapbox: ARGs and How to Appeal to Female Gamers', *Gamasutra.com*. Available: www.gamasutra.com/view/feature/2471/soapbox_args_and_how_to_appeal_to_.php [Accessed 11.01.2019].

Piatt, K. (2009) 'Using Alternate Reality Games to Support First Year Induction with ELGG', *Campus-Wide Information Systems*, 26(4), pp. 313–322.

Sheldon, L. (2011) *The Multiplayer Classroom: Designing Coursework as a Game*, Boston: Cengage Learning PTR.

Unfiction Glossary. (2011) Available: www.unfiction.com/glossary [Accessed 11.01.2019].

Walden, K. (2014) *Searching for District 9 in the Archives: Archaeology of a Transmedia Campaign*, Paper presented at Archives 2.0 Conf.

Walden, K. (2016) 'Nostalgia for the Future: How TRON Legacy's Paratextual Campaign Rebooted the Franchise', in Sara Pesce and Paolo Noto, eds., *The Politics of Ephemeral Digital Media*, London: Routledge, pp. 95–109.

1 Promotional ARGs in context

ARGs are not well-known pieces of kit in the promotional toolbox, perhaps due to their brief lifespan. Their use in marketing campaigns began in 2000, peaking towards the end of the decade. This was significantly affected by the 2008 financial crisis, high running costs, diminishing novelty, and the increasing dominance of cheaper modes of participatory marketing through well-established social media networks. This chapter starts by outlining the structure, rules, and target audiences for promotional ARGs. It then sets the games in a clearer historical context of shifting modes of spectatorship and marketing practices. On the way it introduces three case studies and charts the rise and fall of the genre between 2000 and 2010.

Structures and rules of play

This book does not aim to provide a detailed breakdown of ARG design, but a brief introduction to key elements and terms involved may help navigate the case studies.[1] Askwith (2006: 10) highlights several formal characteristics of ARGs:

1 Unfold across multiple media platforms and real-life spaces
2 Offer an interactive, dispersed narrative experience
3 Require player-participants to reconstruct the dispersed narrative
4 Often refuse to acknowledge themselves as games ("This Is Not A Game")
5 Often have no clear rules or guidelines
6 Often require players to solve difficult challenges or puzzles to progress
7 Often encourage/require the formation of collaborative communities

Transmedia designer Christy Dena adds that ARGs:

1 Respond to player activities through human intervention by "puppetmasters"

2   Are played in real time

(Dena cited in Askwith 2006: 10)

The start of the game is referred to as the 'rabbit hole', a nod to Carroll's *Alice in Wonderland* and the potential oddities of the storyworld into which players are about to tumble. In promotional ARGs for films, this is often hidden in a trailer, poster, official website, or other piece of more traditional marketing. The ensuing narrative usually revolves around a mystery, set in the world of the film, involving events that occur chronologically before or after the film's narrative. In many cases to solve the mystery, you have to see the film. For example, *Cloverfield*'s ARG narrative took players up to the moments before the film's opening sequence, so players essentially had to buy a ticket to find out what happened next.

To push the narrative forward, players must solve puzzles and crack clues of varying styles and difficulty. These can be online (e.g. Flash games, deciphering website passwords) or offline (e.g. large-scale scavenger hunts). Several live events in The Beast and WhySoSerious required players to solve online puzzles to direct players to real-life locations. Live events were highly prized by players and were often built in as finales (see Year Zero [42 Entertainment 2007] and Flynn Lives [42 Entertainment 2009]).[2]

Puzzles are deliberately too complex for one person to complete; they require the collaborative work of the hive mind, or what Jenkins might call the 'knowledge community' (2006: 57). As a result, online communities gather in forums like Unfiction.com. Where there is already a strong fan following (e.g. *The Dark Knight*), multiple player communities can spring up within existing forums, which can be difficult to manage from a producer perspective. As the narrative progresses, players can contact characters and companies in the game via email, phone call, and by post. In-game characters can contact players in the same way. These could be characters established in the film (Commissioner Gordon in *The Dark Knight*) or new characters specifically developed for the game who never appear in the film (Josh Minker in Super 8). The games play out in real time over anything between 3 and 18 months before release. This results in a unique relationship between players and puppetmasters (PMs). PMs must respond quickly to players' actions (or inactions) to keep the game on track, adjusting puzzles, characters, and narrative details. Their real-time, experiential nature gives ARGs a distinctly short shelf life, despite their lengthy duration.[3]

Games usually end with the release of the film, but can continue beyond. *Cloverfield*'s ARG was revived by the DVD release as players continued to look for clues in the film. The game encouraged a mode of 'forensic fandom' (Mittell 2009) as viewers paused, rewound, and replayed the DVD to uncover the origins of the creature that destroyed Manhattan – something neither the film nor ARG explicitly addressed. Whether by design or accident, this enabled the game to drive DVD sales post-release as well as encouraging repeat cinema viewings.

Target audiences

The complexities of ARGs might suggest they appeal only to niche audiences willing to invest the time and effort. It is also tempting to think they appeal primarily to a male adolescent demographic. This can be off-putting for media companies wishing to reach wider audiences, yet Michael Smith (CEO of Mind Candy) claimed participants in *Perplex City* (Mind Candy 2005–2007) included 'plenty of people over 50 years old, and we know that about half of the people who play the game are women' (Smith cited in Askwith 2006: 21).

Askwith (2006) identifies five kinds of ARG players: organisers, hunters, detectives, lurkers, and rubberneckers. The first three are actively involved in puzzle solving and moving the narrative forward, whereas lurkers follow the action without posting. Rubberneckers offer ideas or comments on forums but rarely interact with characters or register their details with in-game websites. Approximately 76% of registered Unfiction players had never or rarely posted on the forums. These players were designated as lurkers, leaving 23% of the community labelled 'active' and only 1% 'highly active' (Figure 1.1). Unfiction estimates the ratio between active players and lurkers to be between 1:5 and 1:20, comprising the majority of an ARG's audience (Unfiction 2011).

Lee emphasises the importance of designing ARGs that engage players on multiple levels (Lee cited in Irwin 2007), envisaging the audience as an inverse triangle:

> The largest broad part at the top is the very, very casual player. There are more of them than anyone else. So, we try to make sure there is at least some easy way into every game we create – a 2–10 minute experience that is rewarding and fun and will hopefully encourage you to come back. . . .

Table 1.1 Unfiction player community activity levels

Player Category	Number of Players	% of Unfiction Community
Lurkers (0–10 posts)	26,074	76%
Active (11–500 posts)	7,600	23%
Highly Active (500+ posts)	317	1%

The middle part is not nearly as populated as the top. Those guys are going to maybe check in every week, every two weeks. We try to make sure they have plenty to do whenever they want to experience it. . . . And then the very tip of the triangle. Those are the crazy guys – the hardcore guys. . . . And the cool thing about this pyramid is there's a really lovely side effect where the bottom part entertains the top parts. . . . And that's just as entertaining. That's like reality TV right there . . . but in order for any one of our experiences to be successful we have to have some mechanism to allow all three of those kinds of players.

(Lee cited in Irwin 2007)

There is a sense of dependency here, yet other designers reflected that media companies were not always interested in reaching the core ARG community, but in 'the ripples that come from what you guys do . . . the people that are lurkers or are reading the news coverage' (Clark 2007). These ripples cannot exist without engaging 'hardcore' players, but this balance is difficult to strike and 2- to 10-minute experiences are significantly cheaper to run than the complicated experiences required to entertain the tip of the triangle.

Rules

There are few set 'rules' to ARGs, but some have developed organically between players and PMs as the genre has evolved, making it somewhat co-creative from inception. Players and PMs agree to adhere to the 'This Is Not A Game' aesthetic (TINAG), whereby the game never acknowledges itself as a game. As much a philosophy as a set of aesthetic guidelines, TINAG requires websites to be convincingly real, phone numbers to actually work, characters to be referred to as if they exist in real life.[4] If PMs have a character do something out of turn to facilitate a narrative twist, the sense of immersion is lost. PMs may not participate in forum conversations as themselves, under pseudonyms, or as characters until the game has ended. If players require further clues, these should be delivered 'in game' rather than through direct forum messages. Posing as characters in an attempt to influence players or 'hijack' the game is forbidden. These rules were eventually formalised on Unfiction and had implications for the relationship between players and PMs. If either side was unable to trust the other to respond appropriately, the game itself became unplayable – for example, if players cheated their way through puzzles or PMs created impossibly difficult puzzles. One PM put this in a neat sporting analogy:

It's very much like a tennis match . . . when that PM team . . . instead of hitting the tennis ball back they hit a bowling ball, it doesn't make sense. . . . If you can't hit the ball back within the court area then players can't play your game.

(Kerr 2007)

This mutual trust is necessary to maintain TINAG. Other media may implicitly require audiences to suspend disbelief, but few set this requirement out so explicitly. ARGs demand more than a suspension of disbelief; they ask players to act upon it, to communicate with characters and follow their instructions as if they were real and as if they matter. To do so requires emotional investment and trust – the greater the investment, the greater the fallout if this proves foolhardy or does not provide an enjoyable experience in return:

> The whole point of an ARG is to engage the audience member in this bizarre 'trust dance', this concept where they want desperately to believe that this stuff is real because it makes it more fun, and the role of an ARG is to do everything in its power to make them not feel stupid about taking that leap with us.

(Lee cited in Siegel 2006)

PMs acknowledged and respected this emotional engagement from players:

> You have to believe that the people who are creating the game you're spending so much time on aren't going to muck you about and play tricks on you, like creating a puzzle that's impossible to solve . . . you are abusing people's trust.

(Hon 2012)

Players demonstrated reciprocal concerns about solving puzzles in a 'proper' manner. 'Brute force' approaches to puzzle solving were discouraged or even condemned on forums. This dynamic might prompt us to reconsider how we conceptualise the relationship between producers and consumers of participatory promotional media. This new configuration also emerged at a time when expectations around audiences' media consumption practices were shifting, including the rise of complex narratives and more active, playful modes of reception.

Context: the rise of gaming, complex narratives, and changing modes of media reception

Askwith (2006) traces forms of immersive entertainment/promotions as far back as Orson Welles' radio adaptation of *War of the Worlds* (1938), which presented the story as a factual newscast. The reaction of audiences is well documented, as millions who tuned in after the disclaimers believed the programme to be a legitimate news report (New York Times 1938; Gosling 2009). He also links ARGs to 'armchair treasure hunts' beginning with *Masquerade* (Williams 1979), a children's book containing clues leading to the secret UK location of a buried jewel. The release of Pink Floyd's album *The Division Bell* in 1994 is cited as the first example of such a game promoting a commercial product (Askwith 2006).[5] Even further back, Fabrice Lyczba (2017) locates immersive marketing strategies in the ballyhoo stunts of 1920s film marketing. These were street media performances ranging from a cardboard *T. rex* paraded through Montgomery, Alabama, to the dumping of 'real Saharan sand' into Times Square in New York, in which audiences were challenged to find buried dollar coins.[6]

This allows us to track a game-playing, mystery-solving, ludically curious media audience throughout the history of film marketing. However, the environment in which promotional ARGs flourished encouraged this participatory mode of engagement on a larger scale, with technological developments playing a pivotal role. The Beast was created in 2001, when high-speed broadband was becoming more readily available to Hollywood's key demographics (youth markets with high levels of disposable income). Immersive or pervasive gaming was not a new development, but online gaming was increasing in popularity. Three successful MMORPGs were released in the late 1990s: *EverQuest* (Sony Online Entertainment 1999), *Ultima Online* (Electronic Arts 1997), and *Ascheron's Call* (Turbine Inc. 1999). All were precursors to contemporary games like *Second Life*, *World of Warcraft*, and *Guild Wars* (AreaNet 2005). Video game takings have been surpassing box office receipts for feature films since 1998 (Caldwell 2008: 277).

The early 2000s also saw a rise in 'casual gaming' enabled by the widespread use of Flash software to produce interactive web pages and online games. This was compounded towards the end of the decade by the increased prevalence of mobile technology and apps, culminating in the enormous popularity of games like *Candy Crush* (King 2012) and *Clash of Clans* (Supercell 2012). Many made their money through in-game microtransactions rather than the heftier prices attached to console games. The industry took this as an indication that not only was the game-playing audience bigger than they had imagined, but they were more than willing to pay to play.[7]

More directly relevant to ARGs was the success of sandbox console games like Rockstar's *Grand Theft Auto* (1997–) series. These proliferated between 2001 and 2010 and promoted the non-linear narrative pleasures of exploring a seemingly endless, unbounded world in which players could experience a multiplicity of narratives in whichever order they chose, moving through the landscape and testing the boundaries of their creativity within the limitations of the sandbox. Some ARGs allowed for a similar experience, for example, exploring the various institutional facets of Gotham City at players' own leisure. In the face of this competition, one might see the uptake of game-like promotions as an attempt by Hollywood to capitalise on the pleasures of gaming that the more linear medium of film could not provide.

The 1990s and early 2000s also saw a movement towards more experimental narrative structures in Hollywood cinema. Examples include *Pulp Fiction* (Quentin Tarantino 1994), *Memento* (Christopher Nolan 2000), *Fight Club* (David Fincher 1999), *Mulholland Drive* (David Lynch 2001), *The Matrix* (Wachowskis 1999), *21 Grams* (Alejandro González Iñárritu 2003), and *Crash* (Paul Haggis 2004). Warren Buckland describes these as films which 'embrace non-linearity, time loops, and fragmented spatiotemporal reality . . . [they] blur the boundaries between different levels of reality, are riddled with gaps, deception, labyrinthine structure, ambiguity and overt coincidences' (2009: 9). This is not to say there were no such films prior to this moment. However, scholars tend to suggest they existed in more 'traditionally difficult' categories of art house and European auteur cinema (Kinder 2002; Elsaesser 2009).

Simons (2008) outlines various labels used to describe this style, including forking path narrative/network narrative (Bordwell 2002, 2008), puzzle films (Panek 2006), mind-game films (Elsaesser 2009), modular narratives (Cameron 2006), multiple draft films (Branigan 2002), database narratives (Kinder 2002), complex narratives (Staiger 2006), and twist films (Wilson 2006). Debates focus on whether they constituted a new era of filmmaking (replacing traditional narrative structures) or were simply a passing trend. However, what is key for ARGs is the active mode of spectatorship required for audiences to make sense of such films. 'Mind-game film' and 'puzzle film' evoke game-playing, and Simons (2008) references game theory and ludology when discussing the reception of their complex temporalities. The simultaneous emergence of ARGs and these game-like films suggests audiences were developing viewing strategies for them and producers were responding to a demand for higher levels of narrative complexity.

Elsaesser suggests these films aim to 'disorient or mislead spectators (besides carefully hidden or altogether withheld information there are frequent plot twists and trick endings)' (2009: 15). However, he argues spectators thoroughly enjoy this challenge. He views the films as responses

> to the conditions of distribution, reception, consumption, cinephilia, connoisseurship and spectatorship appropriate for the multi-platform film, which can seduce a theatre-going public . . . ., engage volatile fan

communities on the internet . . . as well as "work" as a DVD and possibly even as a game.

(2009: 34)

These conditions are specific to shifts in technology, industry, and spectatorship and are all inextricably linked. The latter is most relevant to ARGs, as Elsaesser (2009: 16) argues complex narratives point to 'a crisis in the spectator-film relation . . . the classical spectator positions of "voyeur", "witness", "observer" and their related cinematic regimes or techniques . . . are no longer deemed appropriate, compelling or challenging enough'. The inclusion of an ARG in a film's marketing campaign might be a method of incorporating that complexity without building it into the film itself; an attempt to attract both the emerging 'game-playing' audience and those who did not necessarily desire such a 'challenging' viewing experience.

Elsaesser also mentions fan activity around complex narratives in online forums. He argues such fansites:

either ignore the fictional contract and treat the film as an extension of real life, to which factual information is relevant, or they tend to use the film as a start of the database, to which all sorts of other data – trivia, fine detail, esoteric knowledge – can be added, collected and shared . . . One has to assume that such 'taking for real' is one of the rules of the game that permit participation.

(2009: 35)

This 'taking for real' echoes both the 'This Is Not A Game' (TINAG) philosophy governing ARGs and the collaborative knowledge sharing process and 'forensic fandom' approach required to play. Elsaesser (2009: 19) notes these storytelling strategies have become commonplace in 'mainstream cinema, event-movies/blockbuster, indie films, not forgetting (HBO-financed) television'. Mittell (2006) notes that character and narrative arcs were indeed developing over several episodes, rather than being encased in one. Serial rather than episodic formats became popular in the early 1980s with shows like *Dallas* (CBS 1978–1991) and *Hill Street Blues* (NBC 1981–1987), laying the foundation for narratively complex series including *Twin Peaks* (ABC 1990–1991), *Buffy the Vampire Slayer* (The WB 1997–2001; UPN 2001–2003), *The X Files* (Fox 1993–2018), and *The Sopranos* (HBO 1999–2007). These series frequently violated storytelling conventions, self-consciously bringing attention to narrative mechanisms. Previously, shows provided clear cues for unusual narrative techniques like flashbacks or dream sequences, for fear of disorienting viewers. Complex narratives tend to lack these signals, leaving audiences to decipher it for themselves. This demands a longer-term engagement with the series to allow viewers to learn each show's unique conventions. This 'operational aesthetic' is a pleasure in itself, encouraging audiences to enjoy working out the mechanics behind the diegetic storyworld (2006: 35).

Mittell similarly attributes this narrative style to changes in audience behaviour, developments in media industries, and new technologies. He is careful to note these were not necessarily direct causes, but changes which 'enabled the creative strategies to flourish' (2006: 37). In future essays (2009) he describes these shows as 'drillable' texts, encouraging viewers to take an investigative, detail-oriented approach to their favourite TV shows. He describes this mode of engagement as 'forensic fandom', pointing to the work of *Lost* fans in constructing the Lostpedia – a wiki page that kept a meticulous, analytical eye on the show's narrative and various speculations and fan theories that accompanied it over six series (Mittell 2009).

Producers also started joining online fan discussions to test for viewer understanding and enjoyment; Mittell (2006) cites *Babylon 5* (Warner Bros. 1994–1998) and *Veronica Mars* (UPN 2004–2006; CW 2006–2007) as examples. This indicates a willingness to engage in more active relationships with audiences, pre-empting the relationship between ARG players and producers. Like Elsaesser, Mittell argues:

> The consumer and creative practices of fan culture that culture studies scholars embraced as subcultural phenomena in the 1990s have become more widely distributed and participated in with the distribution means of the internet, making active audience behaviour even more of a mainstream practice.
>
> (2006: 32)

By the early 2000s, the fact that mass audiences had embraced narratives as complex as *Lost* suggested a climate in which media consumers more broadly were ready to engage with the kind of storytelling The Beast could offer.

Case study 1: The Beast – *A.I.: Artificial Intelligence* (Steven Spielberg 2001)

Created in 2001 by a small team at Microsoft Games Studios, The Beast was developed after Microsoft had secured rights to a video game for *A.I.* but were struggling to translate the film into a game.

The team was led by Jordan Weisman (Creative Director of Microsoft's Entertainment division), Sean Stewart (Lead Writer and science fiction novelist), and Elan Lee (Lead Director and Producer) and supported by external teams of programmers, web designers, and artists.[8] Crucially, they instructed anyone with knowledge of the game to deny its existence. The mantra was:

> 'No comment'. We had everybody saying it. Whenever anybody asked them anything about the game, the answer was always 'No Comment'. We had Bill Gates saying it, we had Marketing saying it, we even got Spielberg himself saying 'No Comment'.
>
> (Lee 2002)

This secrecy left the public vaguely aware of the game but starved for information, creating strong media interest. The Microsoft team's description of the game's development suggests a somewhat experimental, creative approach to game content:

> We really had free range on what we wanted to do here. . . . [They] checked in on us every once in a while, but for the most part would find me on my office floor covered in playdough, and just back out of the room shaking their heads. . . .
>
> (Lee cited in Cloudmakers 2001)

The Beast takes place in 2142, 16 years after the events of *A.I.* Global warming has hit a crisis point, leaving New York City submerged by melting ice caps. Humans have created artificial intelligence (A.I.) which exists in several forms including robots, toys, 'living' houses, and programmes running amok in the 'datasphere', a futuristic form of the internet. A.I.s simulate human behaviour and emotions, and as they become more human-like, some feel threatened by their presence (embodied in the Anti-Robot Militia [ARM] movement) while others campaign for their legal rights (reflected in the Coalition for Robot Freedom and militant pro-A.I. factions like BIOS and A,R,I).[9] The story centred around the character Evan Chan, found dead under suspicious circumstances in his A.I. boat,

Cloudmaker. In what appeared to be a basic whodunnit, players were invited to investigate and solve the murder. The narrative is lengthy, intricate, and cannot be adequately represented in this brief case study. It is best understood by reading The Guide, a detailed walkthrough collated by player and forum administrator Adrian Hon (2001).

Starting the game proved more difficult than anticipated, perhaps because the stealthy approach relied on audiences noticing something unusual hidden in the marketing content, rather than making it as obvious as possible. The rabbit hole appeared on 3 March 2001 when the movie poster was distributed and websites went live (Lee 2002). The posters and trailer contained a credit for 'sentient machine therapist' Jeanine Salla. Searching for her name online led to websites including Jeanine's university homepage[10] and Evan Chan's family homepage.[11]

A second entry point was embedded in the words 'Summer 2001', where notches in the text corresponded to a phone number. On calling it, players received a voicemail from a woman who asked them to write to her at thevisionary.net. Visiting thevisionary. net prompted a sound file saying 'Once upon a time, there was a rude and wicked child who came visiting when told to write!' At this point the browser opened a new email message window with an empty address box, the subject line 'I'm so sorry . . .' and a pre-written email signed off: 'your remorseful child'. After some trial and error, it was discovered that on sending this to mother @thevisionary.net, Mother responded with a cryptic email about Jeanine, ending 'she will lead you to Evan just as she led them. . . .' This was designed to prompt players to search for Jeanine Salla and join the game.

When the sites went live, the team were only seeing 10–15 hits per day for the first week (Lee 2002). So, they created a third lead. They took several hard copies of the movie poster and manually circled letters in pen to spell out 'Jeanine is the key' and 'Evan Chan was murdered'. These were sent to several game and entertainment magazine editors. When highly regarded gossip site Ain't It Cool News ran the story, the team saw website hits jump to 20,000 per day (Lee 2002). This kind of detective work did not come as 'naturally' to audiences as PMs had predicted, but soon became their modus operandi. Players scoured websites for clues and created forums to discuss their various speculations. The largest was a Yahoo! Group named Cloudmakers, with around 7,000 registered players. Slowly, a conspiracy theory unravelled as it appeared Chan had uncovered some underhanded dealings at his firm. A variety of characters/suspects emerged, but as each one was ruled out, players returned to the initial corporate conspiracy theory, and finally solved the mystery of his murder.

The Beast was designed to run for six months prior to the film's release, and the team pre-planned three months' worth of game content with three tiers of puzzle difficulty. The Cloudmakers solved it all within 24 hours. Designers were then forced to produce content and respond to players in real time, on the fly (Lee 2002). A development pattern emerged, and players came to anticipate the release of new content on what they termed 'Update Tuesdays', a pattern borne out of necessity as much as design. The resulting game sprawled across 30 websites, 15 phone calls, 35 emails, a fax, and live meet-ups in Chicago, New York, and Los Angeles.

A.I. was released on 29 June 2001, and players were rewarded with a free screening. The game officially ended around a month later when most storylines had been concluded, and players received a heartfelt email from the PMs:

> At this moment, we believe we have been blessed with the best, smartest, most passionate audience imaginable. If you have any questions not covered by the FAQ (coming soon!), or just want to hang out and chat, we will have an electronic get-together at 9 pm EST/ 6 pm PST on Tuesday, July 31.
>
> (www.zone.msn.com/zzzz/auditorium.asp)
> (PM email recorded in Hon 2001)[12]

The get-together mentioned above was documented by players (Cloudmakers 2001) and reflects how keen PMs were to solicit their feedback. If post-game chats or exit polls are still a regular feature of promotional ARGs, they are not practised this openly.

The Beast was hailed as the next big thing in marketing – 'a unique force on the web. The excitement and buzz it created for an online promotion was unheard of' (Boswell 2002). Film marketers had seen something similar in blairwitch.com two years previously. Indeed, Askwith (2006) refers to Campfire's campaign for *The Blair Witch Project* (Daniel Myrick and Eduardo Sánchez 1999) as a precursor to ARGs.[13] Telotte (2001) notes previous film marketing websites amounted to little more than 'electronic press kits', offering information on cast, promotional stills, interviews, and so forth. Blairwitch.com marked a radical departure from this norm, positioning audiences as investigators into the ominous disappearance of three film students. The campaign proved online marketing could have a significant impact on a film's financial success.[14] Moreover, it capitalised on the aforementioned game-playing, mystery-solving, active audience. Telotte argues both the film and blairwitch.com drew on the immersive pleasures of Janet Murray's 'computer-based narratives' (1997), a term covering computer games, navigation of the web and 'hypertexts'. Again, this indicates subtle ways in which Hollywood was looking to the pleasures of an increasingly successful gaming industry. Other interactive film websites emerged for films like *Donnie Darko* (Richard Kelly 2001),[15] but these were single websites rather than sprawling ARGs. The Beast was a genuinely experimental piece of film marketing.

As advertisers struggled to reach online audiences, this early ARG was depicted in trade press as a strategy for 'intelligent', 'creative' companies; a level above those lacking the subtlety, sophistication, and technological know-how to pursue such methods: 'This is what creative marketers were meant to be doing, telling the best stories they could on behalf of clients who trust them to get results' (Boswell 2002). One analyst even claimed film studios were 'starting to get a handle on intellectualising the process of marketing' (Landau 2001). However, the overwhelmingly positive reception of The Beast should be viewed in the context of a period when marketers were struggling to engage a more active, internet-savvy media consumer.

Context: from relationship marketing to virals and beyond

Between 2000 and 2010, marketers were struggling to engage 'new', digitally engaged consumers characterised as inattentive and over-saturated with advertising messages (Goldhaber 1997; Powell 2013); desiring memorable experiences over goods or services (Gilmore & Pine 1998); and active and vocal in their consumption practices (Jenkins 2006). ARGs offered a partial solution to these problems but came with their own issues.

Inattentive consumers – the attention economy

Amid the dot-com boom and bust of the early 2000s, banners and pop-up ads were prominent forms of online advertising. However, these were emphatically 'push' strategies (Powell 2013: 2). They worked by interrupting (Grainge & Johnson 2015) whatever the customer was doing online to sell them a product, experience, or so forth. Ad spends in these areas became higher priorities as broadband connections became more widely available and marketers saw opportunities to reach an audience spending more time and money online.

However, these quickly fell out of favour as it became clear these interruptions were too irritating to be effective. Audiences saturated with advertising simply 'switched off' and, much like television ads were being skipped in the age of TiVo, consumers found ways to avoid, block, and ignore brand messages disrupting their browsing. In the age of the attention economy (Goldhaber 1997), gaining the attention of the increasingly dismissive (or discerning) media audience was as valuable as cash flow.

ARGs offered a significantly more 'pull' approach, with rabbit holes hidden discretely in traditional advertising materials like trailers or posters. Game designer Elan Lee (cited in Ruberg 2006) frequently referenced the subtlety of the address, suggesting 'if, instead of shouting, instead of pushing our message at people, if we whisper it, if we just embed a small flash of imagery in a TV commercial . . . it could be so much more powerful'. PR exposure gained from the 'shoutier' elements, particularly live events, was equally attention-grabbing. Meanwhile, TINAG rules meant the genre came with its own in-built mechanism to keep the advertising message to a whisper. Yet the status of promotional ARGs was always relatively clear. They were linked to existing, recognisable fictional worlds, franchises, or properties, and accessed through 'official' promotional materials like trailers or posters. Those advertising non-narrative products tended to be carefully branded from the outset, for fear of accusations of hoaxing (Dena 2008a) or stealth marketing, which might have damaged consumer trust. For example, Art of the Heist began at the scheduled reveal of the new Audi A3. Instead of the car on the podium, audiences found a message stating the car had been stolen and the public should report any clues to its whereabouts on their (clearly branded) website. Yet, the instruction to treat the game as if it were reality negated that commercial status. This was therefore the perfect way to reach an audience sick of the hard sell (Serazio 2013). Not only did it grab their attention, it sustained it. The average piece of film marketing ranges from a two-second glance at a billboard to an extended trailer of a few minutes. ARGs demand months of dedicated attention.

Grainge and Johnson (2015) note we should not be too quick to buy into the rhetoric of a wholesale shift from 'push' to 'pull', or 'interruption' to 'engagement'. This assumes 'earlier forms of screen advertising were not attempting to engage consumers. Equally it implies that contemporary advertising no longer interrupts' (Grainge & Johnson 2015: 29). They are correct in asserting this shift needs to be understood as discursive – potentially more significant in terms of industry rhetoric than in practice. 'Push' strategies have not been abandoned, and advertisers have and always will be concerned with effectively engaging consumers. However, it was alongside this shift in rhetoric that ARGs emerged, offering something innovative to an industry desperate to find a way past banners and click-throughs.

Experiential consumption – the experience economy

Following Goldhaber's attention economy (1997), Gilmore and Pine published their influential work on the experience economy (1998). Charting an evolution from a goods-based industrial economy to service economy, the authors argue the next logical step is the movement into selling experiences. Powell describes this as the

> commodification of experiences to produce competitive advantage with the concept of authenticity becoming a quality that consumers crave and brands seek to be identified with . . . the point of difference of the product is no longer enough . . . instead this is achieved through involving and interacting with consumers and building your marketing around them.
>
> (2013: 53–54)

The games reflect how companies were 'wrap[ping] experiences around their traditional offering to sell them better' (Gilmore & Pine 1998). Promotional ARGs were often already advertising other media products, meaning they were essentially already embroiled in selling an experience. They developed this by offering the pleasures of gaming, puzzle solving, and live theatre, all in the service of promoting the more linear cinematic experience. They met Gilmore and Pine's criteria of being distinctly personal, memorable events and matched several of their design principles. The experience was necessarily themed around the world of the film; they are often multisensory, particularly in live events; they frequently involve memorabilia (known on player forums as swag) as physical reminders of the experience, for example, 'jokerised' dollar bills found during WhySoSerious.[16] Gilmore and Pine view these items as further products that could command a fee as part of an engaging experience, but in ARGs they serve as prizes or rewards in return for the effective participation of players.

ARGs have yet to answer Gilmore and Pine's call for companies to transition to deliberately designing 'engaging experiences that command a fee' (1998: 98), as most pay-to-play models have failed. However, that call has been answered in the more recent market explosion in experiences like escape rooms, immersive dining experiences, Secret Cinema's immersive film screenings, and Punchdrunk's immersive theatre productions.[17] The promotional ARG is something of a predecessor in that respect, with the experience economy reaching maturity in the 2010s.

Active consumption – from relationship to viral marketing

It appeared the only way to reach the inattentive, experience-craving audience of the early internet was to engage them in a different kind of relationship. That belief persists today as Powell notes 'consumers are no longer marketed "at" but rather engaged in conversation to nurture a personalised relationship with the brand' (Powell 2013: 2). The basic premise of this is not new. Relationship marketing (RM) has been a prominent marketing paradigm for decades, almost universally displacing the four Ps (product, price, place, promotion) (McCarthy 1960) and the marketing mix (Borden 1964).

Rather than focussing on short-term, singular transactions, RM works to establish long-term, loyal customer relationships. More recently, Ben Walmsley (2018) has argued for a reconceptualisation of arts marketing. He claims there has been a paradigm shift away from the product-focussed four Ps model and arts marketers are instead embracing a more audience-focussed, relational four Es model: experience, exchange, environment, and engagement. Walmsley's focus is on the arts and cultural sector as opposed to entertainment, but the idea of building 'meaningful', long-term consumer relationships over short-term transactional ones is prevalent across a range of industries.

Alongside this, Kerrigan highlights a movement away from ideas of value in exchange towards ideas of value in use, 'a notion that value can only be created and acknowledged by the consumer in the act of consumption' (2010: 5). Vargo and Lusch (2006) suggest the consumer is therefore a 'co-creator' of value. This ascribes a more active role to the consumer within the marketing process, rather than being 'somebody to whom something is done!' (Dixon & Blois 1983: 4). Criticisms levelled at RM (Gummesson 1997) tend to suggest this rhetoric is not always enacted in practice, and promises of an equitable relationship between producers and consumers are often left unfulfilled. Chapters 3 and 4 seek to challenge a straightforward interpretation of 'co-creation of value' by questioning precisely how 'active' consumers can be in the context of promotional ARGs and what value is generated from their activity in practice.

RM has historically been difficult (but not impossible) to apply to the film industry due to the disconnect between film producers and their audiences (Kerrigan 2010). Given the close interactions with players, PMs may develop closer relationships with players than the average film marketer is able to have with their audience. Promotional ARGs may be a method of bridging that gap, with PMs functioning as intermediaries, allowing audiences to feel closer to producers. Although they may not lead to the directors or producers, ARGs provide a highly personal channel through which consumers can develop a relationship with the promoted film.

RM is also about creating a dialogue to gain and keep consumer trust. For that dialogue to exist, there must be a higher level of participation and interaction from consumers. However, these conversations were already happening amongst consumers themselves, and marketers needed to find a way into them. They were faced with a 'new' consumer with a

> revised attitude towards consumption . . . fundamentally more demanding and less accepting than their modern counterpart . . . rely[ing] less on traditional promotion and instead positively seek[ing] out information regarding their future purchases.
>
> (Powell 2013: 2)

The need to understand active consumers and their motivations remains at the heart of contemporary marketing strategies. This is not to suggest audiences ever passively received marketing messages. Hall's (1973) encoding/decoding theory can be applied as much to advertising as any other form of cultural communication. Hall theorises the potential for audiences to actively decode alternative or oppositional meanings from those encoded by producers in any given media text. However, with the advent of the internet, consumers' processes of feedback, reviewing, and comparing all became more explicit and visible. A key question was whether this 'potentially empowered the consumer by making markets more transparent and businesses more answerable' (Powell 2013: 1). The term 'potential' here is important. In an era of fake news, branded content, and algorithmically determined and distributed content, we need to be as critical of this discourse of empowerment as possible. Jenkins (2006) argues for the empowered position of the 'knowledge community' or 'collective intelligence'. Collectively, he suggests, online consumers are better positioned to make demands of companies over the production of media texts. The complex power structures of an ARG might challenge this discourse. Their proximity to game producers, the collective intelligence formed within player communities, and their apparent ability to impact the game's narrative suggest ARG players might be empowered to an extent within the confines of the game. Control over textual production in terms of the promoted film is harder to argue for, but the impassioned testimonies of players suggest we could consider empowerment of a different kind, outside the realms of meaning production in the textual sense. Chapter 3 re-evaluates these claims in the context of promotional ARGs, where empowerment may mean different things to different stakeholders.

This tendency to equate 'active' consumers with 'empowered' consumers is also brought into question when we consider ARGs' relationship to viral marketing, with which they are often conflated due to their internet-based origins. As something of a buzzword in the 2000s, viral marketing explicitly recognises an active consumer because 'virality' is only genuinely achieved when the consumer, not the marketer, shares the marketing message and increases word of mouth, whether that's embedded in a GIF, video clip, or URL (Dobele et al. 2005, 2007). Far from empowering consumers, this leads to questions around digital media marketing labour and power, since the audience is performing free marketing work. As unpaid but productive internet users, they are creating surplus value and doing so for free, forming part of what Fuchs terms an internet prosumer commodity which media companies can exploit (Fuchs 2014, 2015). One commentator even described the Cloverfield ARG as 'the ultimate in outsourcing' (Brodesser-Akner 2007). This issue is even more pertinent given that ARGs require a level of participation and emotional investment far beyond sharing a viral video. ARGs never require users to pay, but the transactions between players and producers are not so simple. Chapter 4 asks, Who really benefits from this labour and in what ways? Should this participation be equated to free digital marketing labour? Is this truly exploitative, or an example of media companies providing innovative and creative participatory opportunities for consumers?

Case study 2: WhySoSerious – *The Dark Knight* (Christopher Nolan 2008)

After the success of The Beast, Weisman, Stewart, and Lee founded 42 Entertainment, an LA-based company specialising in immersive marketing experiences. They created high-profile ARGs ilovebees (2004) for *Halo 2* and *Year Zero* (2007), promoting the Nine Inch Nails album of the same name. In 2007, the company launched WhySoSerious for Warner Bros. to promote *The Dark Knight*. The game ran for just over a year, during which players became citizens of Gotham City. The main narrative picked up from the end of the previous instalment in the franchise, *Batman Begins* (Christopher Nolan 2005). Players were recruited to the Joker's mob, causing havoc across Gotham, but could sign up with websites connected to other Gotham institutions, including the police department, press, and political systems. They took part in various tasks for these parties, all of which were revealed to be corrupt on some level.[18] Communities emerged at both Unfiction.com (by now a well-established hub for ARG players) and comic fansite Superherohype.com. 42 Entertainment claims player forums consisted of 400+ threads, 150,000+ posts, and 7 million+ views. The player wiki also reportedly contained 985 total pages, 560 files, and was managed by 386 player-editors.[19]

The rabbit hole was found on 11 May 2007, on official website thedarkknight.warnerbros.com, which linked to Ibelieveinharveydent.com.[20] This led to Ibelieveinharveydenttoo.com, an identical site defaced by the Joker, prompting players to submit their email addresses.[21] As each person signed up, pixels were removed to reveal the first public image of Heath Ledger as the Joker. At Comic-Con on July 26, 'jokerised' $1 bills were scattered across the site in San Diego, leading to whysoserious.com.[22] The site advertised jobs as Joker henchmen and included co-ordinates for a location near the convention with a countdown clock ending at 10am the following day. Players gathered to see a phone number written in skywriting and a mass scavenger hunt began. Prizes included Joker masks and a teaser trailer.

This was the start of several games combining real-world and online interactions. After Thanksgiving, players also received hard copies of The Gotham Times.[23] The paper was posted out and updated online throughout the game. The first edition included a recruitment email address for the Joker: humanresources@ whysoserious.com and clues to sites including the hahahatimes. com[24] (a 'jokerised' version of *The Gotham Times*), gothampolice. com[25], and Wearetheanswer.org (a site requesting tips regarding corrupt GPD officers).[26] Players completed puzzles and tasks for the Joker, campaigned for Gotham's District Attorney candidate Harvey Dent,[27] ran operations with Gotham Police Department (GPD) and supported the caped crusader as part of activist group Citizens for Batman.[28] Each event provided players with rewards, including physical memorabilia, access to unseen film footage, or simply pride in solving the puzzles. A significant number of events were live scavenger hunts, in comparison to the single live event run during The Beast. In addition to the Comic-Con event, players completed a carnival-themed scavenger hunt where they picked up packages from 22 bakeries across the US. These were cakes containing mobile 'joker' phones, which were used to contact players.[29]

Subscribers to US broadband provider Comcast could watch episodes of news programme Gotham Tonight on their on-demand service,[30] which revealed Dent had successfully been elected district attorney. The next issue of the Gotham Times led players to gothamcitypizzeria.com. Sponsored by Domino's, the site offered free pizzas to players in specific locations. The pizza boxes contained codes leading to a secret Citizens for Batman forum, and gothamcablenews.com was updated asking players to submit photos or videos of Batman. Those who did, received Citizens for Batman branded materials including stickers, pins, key rings and t-shirts.

Finally, a countdown timer appeared on citizensforbatman.org, signalling the end of the game on 8 July. After the final tasks for the Joker were completed,[31] players were led to whysoserious.com/ overture,[32] an image of a bomb due to explode on 10 July. At that point, all remaining websites in the game were vandalised by the

Joker.[33] Puzzle pieces on several sites were connected to spell out whysoserious.com/kickingandscreening,[34] where players could apply for free tickets to IMAX screenings of the film, released in the US on 18 July. Anyone who submitted their phone number during the game received a phone call detailing an incident at Gotham National Bank. That incident was revealed in the final episode of Gotham Tonight, when an interview with Dent was interrupted by news that six men wearing clown masks had robbed the bank. Five were killed but one made off with millions. Players would eventually see this scene play out as the opening sequence of *The Dark Knight*.

WhySoSerious is one of the most narratively integrated ARGs to date and is considered to have set the standard for promotional ARGs. It marked a shift in the genre from niche experiment to something more structured that reaches out to wider audiences. It also cemented 42 Entertainment's reputation as the foremost provider of such experiential campaigns, winning them their second Grand Prix award at the Cannes Lions International Advertising Festival. The company were held in high regard by players, who generally had positive responses to '42E'.

WhySoSerious did not share the intricate narrative structure of The Beast and had no mission statement as clear as 'Who killed Evan Chan?' Instead, it allowed players to act on behalf of several characters and institutions, immersing them in Gotham City. It was somewhat episodic, as the game was rigorously structured around tasks or events. The centrality of live events suggests a more pre-planned approach, and in-game cues allowed players to organise themselves before these took place. Events also had specific names, making them readily identifiable to both players and press. This structure was flexible enough to allow players to join at different points in the game with less need for catching up on the narrative. For example, it was possible to register with Harvey Dent's campaign with little knowledge of the Joker's previous activities. WhySoSerious was therefore more appealing to casual players than The Beast, which was harder to join at later stages.

Physical rewards or 'swag' were also more prevalent in WhySoSerious, ranging from Joker phones to Harvey Dent bumper stickers and Citizens for Batman t-shirts. Prizes also included preview screenings of trailers or clips. Stewart (2012) recalls 'eyerolling' when this happened in The Beast, but WhySoSerious players were delighted with these rewards. This increased sense of commerciality affected the relationship between players and PMs. One SHH player felt clues to puzzles from 42 Entertainment were appropriate if posted via 'ninjas' or plants on the forum boards, which was far less acceptable during The Beast. Players also happily contacted 42E directly throughout the game, which technically breaks TINAG. This shift in communication style also reflects changes in perceptions of the PMs. Players increasingly addressed their concerns to '42E', a recognisable corporate entity with a brand reputation which led to players identifying a specific 42E 'style'.

However, any direct comparison with The Beast should consider the context in which WhySoSerious was produced. By 2008, online interactive marketing had become central to film promotion, as opposed to experimental side projects alongside print and broadcast. WhySoSerious is a strong example of an integrated marketing campaign, which was becoming standard procedure for many companies (Powell 2013: 5).

A.I. also lacked the creative baggage which often accompanies a commercially successful franchise. PMs on WhySoSerious were limited as to the kinds of worlds, storylines, and characters they could create. Gotham City had already been outlined both aesthetically and thematically in *Batman Begins*, taking the comic book adaptation in a less stylised, darker, and more violently realistic direction than predecessors Tim Burton and Joel Schumacher. *The Dark Knight* also focussed heavily on the reintroduction of the Joker and Two-Face as old-but-new characters who had undergone significant transformations. The reboot was thus faced with managing expectations of not only an enormous, historic Batman fanbase, but also cinema audiences more broadly. These characters would have been familiar even to casual moviegoers, who may still have come to *The Dark Knight* with previous experience of Batman films. There was significantly less room for creative experimentation than there had been with The Beast.

In comparison, The Beast's creative baggage was lightweight, despite concerns from fans over the project's transferral to Spielberg after Kubrick's death. The world and story material were entirely original and shrouded in such secrecy that expectations were less clearly defined and therefore easier to manage. Why-SoSerious was more heavily burdened with commercial responsibilities and was therefore a more commercially managed affair.

2008–2011: peak to decline

The mid 2000s saw a flurry of high-profile promotional ARGs, including Audi's Art of the Heist (2005), the Lost Experience (2006), and Year Zero (2007).[35] At this point the Wikipedia article entitled 'History of Alternate Reality Games' ends somewhat abruptly. Yet 2008 arguably saw a 'peak' moment for promotional ARGs. Abrams' first feature film *Cloverfield* was preceded by the game 1–18–08, eagerly anticipated by fans of *Alias* and *Lost*. The same year, MacDonald's launched The Lost Ring ARG in conjunction with the 2008 Olympic Games and the British Red Cross ran a game called Traces of Hope, in which players were tasked with reuniting a Ugandan teenager with his mother during civil war.

Trade press coverage oscillated between describing ARGs as the 'future of marketing' or a 'long term strategic tool' (Readon 2009) and warning against it as short-sighted bandwagon-jumping. As a result, a myriad of claims were made for their effectiveness. They were praised for being cost-effective (Smith 2008; Weisman cited in Kyllo 2009), yet this was difficult to ascertain since reports around production costs were often vague or dealt in large figures for high-profile games. This could be attributed to general excitement around the cost-saving implications of viral marketing. One article claimed it could be '15 times more effective than ads posted on the net and much cheaper – no costly billboards or TV airtime, just focused free-to-air word of mouth' (Watson 2001). Since ARGs often promoted highly anticipated films, TV shows, or console games with existing fanbases, box office takings were not necessarily a clear-cut indicator of success either. PR and press coverage were often more important for these products: 'column inches are the win, they were going to sell $100m of *Halo* on the first day' (Stewart 2012).

Tron Legacy (2010) is perhaps the last mainstream Hollywood film to use a large-scale promotional ARG, also run by 42 Entertainment. Impressive in its scope, Flynn Lives involved several spectacular live events, including the recreation of Flynn's arcade and a Live Encom 'Press Conference' which was disrupted when Sam Flynn parachuted in from a helicopter.[36] The final event saw 7,000 visitors experience a recreation of the End of the Line Club where a trailer was shown on an immersive screen. It demonstrated, like WhySoSerious, the value of such tactics to established franchises with an existing fanbase to court. However, these declined in favour of smaller-scale viral campaigns which arguably offered reduced levels of interaction and immersion, along with less intricate storytelling. Examples ranged in terms of complexity. *Fifty Shades of Grey* (Sam Taylor-Johnson 2015) encouraged audiences to apply for internships at Grey Enterprises.[37] Fans created LinkedIn-style profiles and completed basic online tasks which usually required them to share their activities via social media to progress to the next level or access bonus content.[38] Similarly, players created employee profiles for *Jurassic World* (Colin Trevorrow 2015) bioengineering corporation Ingen. The theme park's site offered more in the way of interactivity, multimedia content, and worldbuilding. It was eventually hacked by the Dinosaur Protection Group, which also had a strong online presence.[39] Finally, Grainge and Johnson (2015) describe the multi-layered campaign for the *Hunger Games* franchise. Again, users created a profile and were assigned a District, positioning them as oppressed inhabitants of Panem.[40] They then witnessed the uprising that unfolds during the franchise across every conceivable social media channel, receiving enormous amounts of content. Yet even in this campaign, interaction was comparatively low and narratives less complex than in WhySoSerious or Flynn Lives. The age of the full-blown ARG had seemingly passed.

For media companies, there are any number of reasons not to commission promotional ARGs. Large-scale games and live events are costly and logistically difficult to run. The games are labour intensive, requiring a committed team of PMs to work long hours to respond to player movements. Having made that investment in labour and event collateral, the return on investment (ROI) on a promotional game is difficult to discern. This became even more off-putting after the financial crash in 2008, which saw advertising budgets tighten across industries including Hollywood (*The Economist* 2009). Reports around initial production costs were also vague: 'It's a question of how long is a piece of string. It depends who you work with, how complex the game is, how many resources you need' (Alice Taylor cited in Smith 2008). When numbers were mentioned, these ranged from '7 figure propositions' (Stewart 2012) for large-scale games to 'well below $1,000,0000' (Gallagher 2001), 'x hundred thousand, half a million' (Hon 2012), or 'anywhere from 50–500k' (Christiano 2013). Yet ARGs were often pitched as better value in comparison to print or broadcast campaigns (Smith 2008; Weisman cited in Kyllo 2009).

Measuring success by reach is equally difficult. Table 1.2 describes the varying statistics used to indicate a successful ARG.

Table 1.2 ARG engagement statistics: The Beast, ilovebees, and WhySoSerious

	The Beast	ilovebees	WhySoSerious
Participants	3 million people actively participated.[1] Cloudmakers numbered in excess of 7,500 (Hoxsey 2005). 2.5 million players (Dena 2008b).	3 million players.[2] 10,000 beekeepers were mobilised in public, 600,000 were actively solving puzzles online, and 2.3 million were keeping tabs on the plot (Hoxsey 2005; Landau 2001).	Over 11 million unique participants in over 75 countries.[3] More than 10 million participants.[4] 750,000–800,000 participants engaged in real-world activities in 380 cities worldwide.[5] 'The 12-hour cake hunt involved only a few dozen people on the ground but some 1.4 million gathered online to see what would happen' (Rose 2011: 10–13).
Traffic/Social	300 million impressions.[6] 1 million unique users, more than 3 million sessions, with 28% of visitors remaining online for more than half an hour (Landau 2001).	500,000+ unique hits on ilovebees. com per day (Dena 2008b). 2,000,000+ recorded unique hits on an update day (Dena 2008b).	1,300 videos and 5,000 photos related to the campaign posted on YouTube and Flickr.[7]

1. http://web.archive.org/web/20120930005458/http://www.42entertainment.com/beast.html
2. http://www.42entertainment.com/work/ilovebees
3. Statistics from 42 Entertainment Promotional Video http://www.42entertainment.com/work/whysoserious
4. Statistics from 42 Entertainment Promotional Video http://www.42entertainment.com/work/whysoserious
5. Statistics from 42 Entertainment Promotional Video - http://www.42entertainment.com/work/whysoserious
6. http://web.archive.org/web/20120930005458/http://www.42entertainment.com/beast.html
7. Statistics from 42 Entertainment Promotional Video http://www.42entertainment.com/work/whysoserious

These are all large-scale but cannot convey engagement on a more nuanced level. Many promotional ARGs will not hit the audience numbers Hollywood expects for a blockbuster. However, despite incorporating qualitative audience engagement data into evaluations, these metrics are still widely used within the industry, and designers must work within that system to prove an ARG's worth to clients. It's a hard sell for executives, despite designers insisting the games can allow for different levels of involvement (Lee cited in Irwin 2007). Realistically, a small core will engage intensely, and most will be fans who would have bought tickets to opening weekend regardless. There are strong arguments for the effectiveness of these strategies for brand management and engaging productively with fan audiences, but they will not put bums on seats. ARGs also no longer command the column inches they once did: 'By the time we were finishing ilovebees [2004] the techniques of The Beast had become ubiquitous . . . it was like yeah, seen it, it's a marketing thing. . . . I'm not gonna give you press for some marketing thing' (Stewart 2012).

As the genre developed, the barrier to entry for an ARG became too severe for corporate clients. The Beast had set the bar too high, and although clients were keen to meet the perceived need for active audience engagement, Christiano (2013) suggests more complex projects were financially and logistically too complicated and required too much commitment. Instead, marketers started looking for something with a smaller scale and budget, but a similar level of impact:

> The full on Deep Dive just requires so much time and so many resources for a dubious ROI. . . . A lot of people in movies are trying to come up with things that are less ornate but still get some of the value.
>
> (Stewart 2012)

We then see a distinct shift from complex puzzles and storyworlds, focussed on a core group of players, to simpler puzzles, designed for broader audiences. According to Jenkins' (2006) theory, more players should mean more collective intelligence, allowing for more difficult puzzles. However, in the case of ARGs, more players usually means more casuals, who are assumed to require an easier game to keep them engaged. This suggests a tension between the games-as-games and games-as-marketing, with designers finding it difficult to create a balanced experience to please dedicated players as well as wider audiences. Complexity starts to be exchanged for accessibility and arguably commerce begins to trump creativity.

This is not to suggest complicated cross-media or transmedia promotional paratexts no longer exist. They have specific value for fan audiences, and it's in these cases that campaigns might become more ARG-like. For example, Hardy (2013) argues the *Prometheus* campaign is a prime example of a synergistic, corporate cross-media campaign. It would not be considered an ARG, as the game-like, ludic elements are not present. It is, however, an incredibly effective, complex piece of transmedia storytelling delivered through a cross-media marketing campaign aimed squarely at fans of the franchise who want to dive deeper.

Viral campaigns, in contrast, work towards solving these problems whilst retaining some of the interactivity of a full-blown ARG. Reducing (but not removing) agency reduces logistical and financial risk. The increased integration of social networks like Facebook, Twitter, and Instagram produces more measurable, reportable engagement data using existing industry metrics. It thus becomes easier to argue for positive ROI. Potentially viral content is also put before a mass audience in spaces which are semi-personal but do not encroach on dedicated fan spaces like forums or fan-created websites. Such social networks are occupied by fans and non-fans alike, allowing word of mouth to spread more efficiently to wider audiences rather than being confined to fan communities. These adjustments make the content significantly more accessible. Powell claims from about 2005 the 'mediascape of the web became fundamentally social' (Han 2011: 5). ARGs were able to capitalise on this to some extent, but it's worth remembering that The Beast, *Majestic*, and *Alias* ARGs all launched four years before Facebook even existed (see Figure 1.3).

Larger-scale, high-profile games ran between 2004 and 2010. During this time Facebook (2004), YouTube (2005), and Twitter (2006) were launched but had not yet embedded themselves into everyday life or promotional culture in the manner we see today. Smartphones and mobile devices were developing, but were by no means commonplace. ARGs therefore worked predominately in an online space best described as a nascent Web 2.0 environment, relying on player-constructed forums and email to reach audiences. Arriving in 2010, two years after WhySoSerious but two years before *Prometheus*, *Super 8*'s campaign started to indicate the changing direction of promotional ARGs.

Case study 3: Super 8 – *Super 8* (J.J. Abrams 2011)

In the time between 2001 and 2010, the web had become a very different space. The proliferation of personal profiles enabled by Web 2.0 and social media channels made it easier for marketers to utilise established social networks to spread a message 'virally'. In Hollywood, new generations of filmmakers not only shared the cinephilia of predecessors like Spielberg and Lucas, but also were well-versed in web culture and transmedia storytelling, with clearer ideas about the online representation and dissemination of their work. What was new, unexplored territory for the *A.I.* team was now more firmly mapped out and easier to navigate.

This was particularly true for J.J. Abrams. He had already written and produced two TV series with ARGs attached (*Alias* and *Lost*),

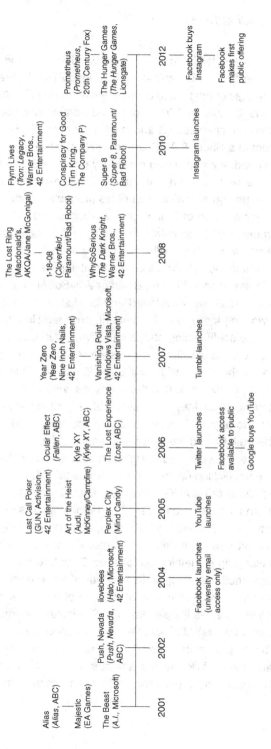

Figure 1.3 ARG/social media timeline

both well known for intricate, mysterious plots. In 2008 he produced *Cloverfield*, which entailed a year-long ARG.[41] Abrams had also (knowingly or otherwise) constructed an image of himself as a PM of sorts; Christiano (2013) confirmed Abrams was particularly involved in concept meetings and in all final approvals. Fans therefore expected a Super 8 ARG, and by 2010 the player community had expanded, the genre was more fully developed, and the hive mind was ready and waiting. Abrams therefore needed to maintain his own reputation as well as that of his production company, Bad Robot. Originally part of Touchstone Television, Bad Robot moved with Abrams in 2006 to establish long-term contracts with Paramount and Warner Bros. Whether this relationship affected the development of the ARG is uncertain, but it implies a different production context than either The Beast or WhySoSerious.

Super 8's ARG was developed and produced by various contractors working for Amblin, Paramount, and Bad Robot. The film is a nostalgic sci-fi/coming-of-age narrative, set in Lillian, Ohio, in the 1970s. A group of children witness a terrifying train crash whilst making a zombie movie with their Super 8 camera. They discover their teacher Dr Woodward in the wreckage, who warns them not to tell anyone what they have seen. Shortly afterwards strange things start to happen in town, so Joe, Alice, and Charles set out to find the truth behind the train's mysterious cargo.

ARG players were based at Unfiction.com and cloverfieldclues. blogspot.com, picking up the same audience from the Lost Experience and *Cloverfield*'s ARG. The game initially followed a recognisable pattern for seasoned players. The rabbit hole was embedded in a teaser trailer released in May 2010, and players were eagerly waiting to sift through it frame by frame. The trailer depicted the train transporting something out of Area 51 before the crash, followed by something punching its way out of the wreckage. Slowing down the flickering film reel at the end of the trailer revealed the phrase 'scariestthingieversaw'. Scariestthingieversaw.com (STIES) was the first ARG website and launched the first of three discernible strands of the campaign, all set in present day.

The first strand followed the attempts of new character Josh Minker to unravel his father's role in the events of the film. Players followed communications on STIES, a remote PC desktop, as Josh is contacted by an anonymous informant who they dubbed 'Mysterio'.[42] He claimed to have information on Josh's father's whereabouts and his involvement in the government cover-up of the creature on the train.[43] Clues led players to Josh's blog[44] and conspiracy site revalistic.com.[45] The answers seemed to rest with a mysterious object referred to as the 'vitas relic'. Josh's house was raided by his colleague Sarah and her team, who were also looking for the relic. Mysterio was eventually tracked down by the authorities and left a farewell note indicating he had taken his own life rather than being tortured into sharing information. After a long pause, an update from Josh informed players that both he and Sarah were safe and had found the vitas relic, which was a cube of some kind (identified later as an Argus cube and significant in the film). He eventually found his father's grave in Lillian, along with a note explaining that after a confrontation with the alien creature, Mr Minker had become obsessed with finding it again, changed his name, and moved frequently. In the film, it emerged that Dr Woodward was in fact Josh's father. He caused the train crash to help the alien escape the clutches of the government. This seemed to conclude the narrative, but still left questions unanswered.

The second strand of the ARG also originated with the STIES site. It prompted players to print a newspaper document which directed them to RocketPoppeteers.com, a website for a fictional ice-lolly brand with mini-games, challenges, and merchandise.[46] Rocket Poppeteers ice cream trucks were also spotted at Comic-Con, announced via their Twitter account.[47] The site wound down around June 2011 when the five top-scoring players in the mini-games were rewarded with recognition on a scoreboard and a collectible Argus cube.[48] Rocket Poppeteers had little interaction with the rest of the ARG, although players searched for connections.

The third strand of the game appeared when the first full trailer was released in March 2011, via the official website.[49] Designed to look like an editing room with hanging filmstrips, players were encouraged to unlock missing frames via Twitter and create a clip. Websites including Wired.com and Slashfilm.com were sent packages with a strip of Super 8 film, a USB stick containing a black and white film clip, and a card with a code and email address. Emailing the code back to the sender unlocked a frame in the Editing Room. Players also unlocked frames by signing up to the Super 8 Development Room via Facebook and logging in at specific times in the run-up to release. This entered them into a prize draw for Super 8 t-shirts and film strips including their unlocked frame. Frames were also hidden in the Super8 iPhone/iPad app and cinema standees. The final clip was an incident report from government experiments, involving the recovery and study of an alien spacecraft, the creature, and its technology, including energy-generating Argus cubes. None of this thread was recorded on the Super 8 wiki page, suggesting players did not deem this part of the ARG proper, but a separate viral element of the campaign.[50]

The Josh Minker narrative could be referred to as the ARG 'proper' and had some intersection with the Editing and Development Rooms. Rocket Poppeteers was relatively stand-alone and echoed previous fictional brands in Abrams ARGs.[51] Beginning with a conspiracy theory premise, the game engaged players quickly. However, as it continued it broke with existing ARG norms and developed a less clearly defined role within the rest of the marketing campaign, leading to mixed reactions from players. Loose ends were tied together hastily, and characters felt underdeveloped. Sites such as revalistic.com, with its abundance of conspiracy theories and scientific information, prompted lots of player speculation but rarely confirmed it.

The loose connections between the three strands often made the game hard to follow as a singular entity. Having developed a reputation for red herrings and dead ends in *Lost*, fans were not surprised to find them in the Super 8 ARG: *'Going by previous projects of the Master of Mystery JJ Abrams, Super 8 will probably spawn a LOT of speculation'* (UF).

However, one review expresses frustration succinctly:

I enjoyed the game very much, but I thought it ended rather abruptly. I was very unsatisfied, as it was too quick and anticlimactic. We never learn who is after Josh, what that energy was that saved Sarah, and why Woodward [Josh's father] even wanted Josh to find the vitas relic. This felt like the *Lost* finale without the emotional climax to make up for not giving us all the answers.

(Koelsch 2011)

Elsaesser's (2009) game-playing audiences may enjoy being toyed with, but they still desire traditional narrative closure. The game formally ended with the US release of the film on 10 June 2011, but additional online content appeared to time with international release dates and it is unclear whether this was designed to continue the story. The Rocket Poppeteer thread kept players occupied, but updates to the Minker narrative became few and far between, frustrating players who felt the story was not progressing. This may have been a player management strategy, keeping them starved for information until the last minute. However, disgruntled forum discussion suggests this was not necessarily effective.

Project C were responsible for the Editing Room and Development Rooms as well as scariestthingieversaw.com. Rocket Poppeteers was run by Watson D/G. Both companies previously provided content for other Paramount/Bad Robot properties, including *Cloverfield* and *Star Trek* (2009). However, their services are more diverse than that of 42 Entertainment, ranging from 'all-encompassing web campaigns'[52] to individual viral elements for campaigns, web content, and strategy for digital marketing initiatives. Project C's section of the ARG was developed around video content provided by Abrams and the team were charged with delivering that content in 'a cool way . . . in small chunks that also engaged the audience in a collaborative effort' (Christiano 2013). Beyond this, they were offered little guidance, similarly to The Beast: 'We were given the idea and then a ton of rope to go make it happen somehow' (Christiano 2013). Trade press continued to express ambiguity around ARGs:

> A couple of years ago clients were asking for virals, then blogs, then UGC [user generated content] campaigns. I do feel that alternate reality games are a bit of a fad right now. If agents and clients do it blindly just because it's the buzzword then it'll just lead to copycat tactics.
>
> (Rei Inamoto cited in Goldie 2008)

Meanwhile, an entire industry had emerged around transmedia storytelling, including ARGs. Pressure was therefore on developers to keep the genre fresh, innovative, and involving. Producers were required to prove its long-term effectiveness to secure contracts for campaigns.

Conclusion

Promotional ARGs emerged and declined in a specific context of historical, technological, and industrial change. Difficulty defining them often stems from their blurring of several boundaries: fiction/reality, commerce/creativity, marketing/storytelling, online/offline gaming. They perform dual functions as pieces of creative, transmedia storytelling on one hand, and commercially oriented marketing materials on the other. Evidently, they can and do perform both roles but remain unique forms of both, offering an interactive, immersive, and affective narrative experience.

Enabled to an extent by the increased availability of broadband internet connections, promotional ARGs appealed to marketers trying to reach 'new' consumers who were spending more time online. They offered a version of online marketing beyond banner ads and pop-ups to reach a consumer defined by the industry as active (Dixon & Blois 1983; Jenkins 2006), short in attention span (Goldhaber 1997), and increasingly viewing experiences as more valuable than products (Gilmore & Pine 1998). From an audience perspective, they offered a mode of storytelling that appealed to viewers looking for something more challenging and interactive than traditional linear narratives. This game-playing, inquisitive, and forensically minded audience was already experiencing increased narrative complexity in mainstream film and television and was therefore perfectly positioned to take interest in games like The Beast.

The three case studies introduced in this chapter demonstrate the gradual development of the genre over roughly ten years, as ARGs became less of an experimental novelty and more embedded within marketing campaigns for major Hollywood film franchises. Their decline after 2010 can be attributed to several factors including reduced marketing budgets, difficulty proving ROI, and lack of novelty. Smaller-scale viral campaigns linked to ready-made audiences on social networks proved less risky and easier to quantify. Large-scale promotional games such as Flynn Lives therefore tended to be launched for established franchises with large, pre-existing fanbases who were more likely to engage more deeply with the games. The next chapter explores the position of the case studies in relation to the films they promoted, their integration within wider marketing campaigns, and their function as promotional materials.

Notes

1 Several publications address ARG design in more depth (Szulborski 2005; Hansen et al. 2013; Evans 2014).
2 www.42entertainment.com/work/yearzero
  www.42entertainment.com/work/flynnlives
3 See Janes 2016 for further discussion of the varying temporalities simultaneously at work in promotional ARGs.
4 See Janes 2017 for a more detailed examination of TINAG.
5 A Usenet group member started posting messages referring to himself as Publius. He suggested an 'enigma' was hidden in the album and that there was a reward for the first person to solve it.
  Although other fans were sceptical, Publius was proven right when he correctly predicted that white lights would appear on the stage at a New Jersey concert, spelling out PUBLIUS ENIGMA. The enigma remains unsolved and the prize unclaimed (Askwith 2006).
6 Promotions for *The Lost World* (Harry Hoyt 1924) and *When the Desert Calls* (Ray C. Smallwood 1922) respectively.
7 The audience was also more female than they realised. See Eklund 2016 for discussions around gender in the casual gaming market.
8 Credits mention Three Mountain Group, Atomic Pictures, Field-Y, and Code Ring https://groups.yahoo.com/neo/groups/cloudmakers-moderated/conversations/messages/1019 [Accessed 28.03.2019]
9 Players speculated whether these might have been computing in-jokes from Microsoft, referring to the Basic Input/Output System and common prompt 'Abort, Retry, Ignore'.
10 Jeanine's university homepage: http://web.archive.org/web/20060105074034/http://bangaloreworldu-in.co.cloudmakers.org/salla/default.html
11 Evan Chan's family homepage: http://web.archive.org/web/20060105143842/http://familychan.cloudmakers.org/evanchanpage.html
12 http://web.archive.org/web/20060105103026/http://cloudmakers.org/guide/index4.shtml#10.2puppet
13 The team at Campfire went on to launch the ARG Art of the Heist for Audi and promotions for HBO's *True Blood* (Hardy 2011).
14 On a budget of $60,000, *The Blair Witch Project* grossed nearly $250 million globally at the box office.
15 See Beck 2004.
16 http://batman.wikibruce.com/Image:Jokerdollar.jpg
17 www.secretcinema.org/
  www.punchdrunk.org.uk/
  www.thevaults.london/divine-proportions
  www.time-run.com/
18 The reel for this on 42 Entertainment's website gives a flavour of the complexity of the game. www.42entertainment.com/work/whysoserious
19 www.42entertainment.com/work/whysoserious
20 http://batman.wikibruce.com/Ibelieveinharveydent.com

21 http://batman.wikibruce.com/Ibelieveinharveydenttoo.com
22 http://batman.wikibruce.com/Whysoserious.com
23 http://batman.wikibruce.com/Image:GothamTimesPapers.jpg
24 https://web.archive.org/web/20081219183655/www.thehahahatimes.com:80/
25 http://web.archive.org/web/20071125174343/www.gothampolice.com:80/
26 http://web.archive.org/web/20080508212459/www.wearetheanswer.org:80/
27 www.whysoseriousredux.com/dent/ibihd/home.htm
28 http://web.archive.org/web/20080330102647/www.citizensforbatman.org:80/
29 http://batman.wikibruce.com/Image:Cake.jpg
    http://batman.wikibruce.com/Image:Insides.jpg
    http://batman.wikibruce.com/Image:Package.jpg
30 http://batman.wikibruce.com/Gotham_Tonight
31 http://web.archive.org/web/20090322192653/www.whysoserious.com:80/
32 http://batman.wikibruce.com/Whysoserious.com/Overture
33 https://web.archive.org/web/20090107013234/http://gothampolice.com/
    http://web.archive.org/web/20090405000236/www.citizensforbatman.org:80/
34 http://batman.wikibruce.com/Whysoserious.com/Kickingandscreening
35 https://en.wikipedia.org/wiki/History_of_alternate_reality_games
36 www.42entertainment.com/work/flynnlives
37 http://web.archive.org/web/20150430002107/www.greyenterprisesholdings.
    com:80/
38 www.stradellaroad.com/work/fifty-shades-of-grey
39 http://islanublar.jurassicworld.com/dinosaurs/
40 www.thecapitol.pn/
41 Cloverfield does not feature as a case study as it was released in the same year
    as WhySoSerious. Super 8 provides an example of a more recent Abrams ARG.
42 http://super8.wikibruce.com/Scariestthingieversaw.com
43 A walkthrough of the desktop in use can be found here: www.youtube.com/
    watch?v=yXKF-qmrbUU
44 http://web.archive.org/web/20100705082938/www.hooklineandminker.com:80/
45 http://web.archive.org/web/20110308022402/http://revalistic.com:80/
46 http://super8.wikibruce.com/Rocketpoppeteers.com
47 https://twitter.com/RocketPoppeteer
48 http://super8.wikia.com/wiki/Argus_Cubes
    http://s302.photobucket.com/user/mach1monorail/library/ARGUS%20Cube?
    sort=3&page=1
49 www.super8-movie.com/editingroom.html
50 http://super8.wikibruce.com/Home
51 Abrams fans would have seen a fictional soft drink called Slusho in *Cloverfield* and
    Alias ARGs. The Poppeteer website references Slusho by citing its mysterious and
    addictive main ingredient (kaitei no mitsu) in the ingredients of one of the lollies.
52 www.behance.net/watsondg

References

Askwith, I. (2006) *This Is Not (Just) an Advertisement: Understanding Alternate Real-
    ity Games*, MIT Convergence Culture Consortium White Paper. Available: http://
    convergenceculture.org/research/c3_not_just_an_ad.pdf [Accessed 11.01.2019].
Batman Begins (2005) dir. Christopher Nolan.

Beck, J. C. (2004) 'Concept of Narrative: An Analysis of Requiem for a Dream (.com) and Donnie Darko (.com)', *Convergence: The International Journal of Research into New Media Technologies*, 10(3), pp. 55–82.

Borden, N. H. (1964) 'The Concept of the Marketing Mix', *Journal of Advertising Research*, 4, pp. 2–7, June.

Bordwell, D. (2002) 'Film Futures', *Substance*, 31(1), pp. 88–104.

Bordwell, D. (2008) *Poetics of Cinema*, New York, NY: Routledge.

Boswell, K. (2002) 'Telling Good Stories: How the AI Online Campaign Kicked Viral Marketing Over the Fence to Us All', *The Marketleap Report*, 2(4). Available: www.marketleap.com/report/ml_report_23.htm [Accessed 24.06.2009]. No longer available online. Print copy held by author.

Branigan, E. (2002) 'Nearly True: Forking Plots, Forking Interpretations. A Response to David Bordwell's "Film Futures"', *Substance*, 31(1), pp. 105–114.

Brodesser-Akner, C. (2007) 'Only Gumshoes Can See This Movie', *Advertising Age*, 78(28) pp. 4–36.

Buckland, W. (2009) 'Introduction', in W. Buckland ed., *Puzzle Films*, Malden, MA; Oxford: Wiley-Blackwell.

Caldwell, D. (2008) *Production Culture: Industrial Self Reflexivity and Critical Practice in Film and Television*, Durham, NC: Duke University Press.

Cameron, A. (2006) 'Contingency, Order and the Modular Narrative: 21 Grams and Irreversible', *The Velvet Light Trap*, 58, pp. 65–78, Fall.

Christiano, J. (2013) *Email Interview with Author*, 06.03.2013.

Clark, B. (2007*) ARGFest Transcript 03 – Panel 1 – Developing an ARG*. Available: https://web.archive.org/web/20080331221502/http://wiki.argfestocon.com/index.php?title=2007vt03_Transcription [Accessed 05.01.2019].

Cloudmakers (2001) *Post-Game Puppetmaster Chat*, 31.07.2001. Available: http://groups.yahoo.com/neo/groups/cloudmakers/files [Accessed 11.01.2019].

Dena, C. (2008a) *Anti Hoaxing Strategies and the TINAG Fallacy*. Available: www.christydena.com/2008/01/anti-hoaxing-strategies-and-the-tinag-fallacy/ [Accessed 17.01.2019].

Dena, C. (2008b) *ARG Stats*. Available: www.christydena.com/arg-stats/ [Accessed 11.03.2019].

Dixon, D. & Blois, K. (1983) 'Some Limitations of the 4 P's as a Paradigm for Marketing,' in *Back to Basics, Proceedings of the Marketing Education Group*, Cranfield School of Management, pp. 92–107.

Dobele, A., Toleman, D. & Beverland, M. (2005) 'Controlled Infection! Spreading the Brand Message Through Viral Marketing', *Business Horizons*, 48(2), pp. 143–149.

Dobele, A. et al. (2007) 'Why Pass on Viral Messages? Because They Connect Emotionally', *Business Horizons*, 50(4), pp. 291–304.

Donnie Darko (2001) dir. Richard Kelly.

The Economist. (2009) 'Nothing to Shout About', *The Economist*, 30.07.2009. Available: www.economist.com/business/2009/07/30/nothing-to-shout-about [Accessed 17.01.2019].

Eklund, L. (2016) 'Who Are the Casual Gamers? Gender Tropes and Tokenism in Game Culture', in W. Willson & T. Leaver, eds., *Social, Casual and Mobile Games*, New York, NY: Bloomsbury.

Elsaesser, T. (2009) 'The Mind-Game Film', in Warren Buckland, ed., *Puzzle Films*, Malden, MA; Oxford: Wiley-Blackwell.

Evans, E. (2014) '"We're All a Bunch of Nutters!" The Production Dynamics of Alternate Reality Games', *International Journal of Communication*, 8(1), pp. 2323–2340.

Fifty Shades of Grey (2015) dir. Sam Taylor-Johnson.

Fuchs, C. (2014) *Digital Labour and Karl Marx*, New York, NY: Routledge.

Fuchs, C. (2015) *Culture and Economy in the Age of Social Media*, New York, NY: Routledge.

Gallagher, D. F. (2001) 'Some Prefer Online "A.I." Tie-In to the Movie', *The New York Times*, 9.07.2001. Available: www.nytimes.com/2001/07/09/technology/09GAME.html [Accessed 05.01.2015].

Gilmore, J. & Pine, J. (1998) 'Welcome to the Experience Economy', *Harvard Business Review*, 07–08.1998.

Goldhaber, M. (1997) 'The Attention Economy and the Net', *First Monday*, 2(4), 04.1997. Available: www.firstmonday.org/article/view/519/440.

Goldie, L. (2008) 'Copycat Warning Over Alternative Reality Games', *New Media Age*, pp. 1–2, 9.10.2008

Gosling, J. (2009) *Waging the War of the Worlds: A History of the 1938 Radio Broadcast and Resulting Panic*, Jefferson, NC: McFarland & Co.

Grainge, P. & Johnson, C. (2015) *Promotional Screen Industries*, London; New York, NY: Routledge.

Gummesson, E. (1997) 'Relationship Marketing as a Paradigm Shift: Some Conclusions from the 30R Approach', *Management Decision*, 35(4), pp. 267–272.

Hall, S. (1973) *Encoding and Decoding in the Television Discourse*, Birmingham: The University of Birmingham, Birmingham Centre for Contemporary Cultural Studies.

Han, S. (2011) *Web 2.0*, London; New York, NY: Routledge.

Hansen, D., Bonsignore, E., Ruppel, M., Visconti, A. & Kraus, K. (2013) 'Designing Reusable Alternate Reality Games', *Proceedings of the SIGCHI Conference on Human Factors in Computing Systems*, pp. 1529–1538, 27.04.2013.

Hardy, J. (2011) 'Mapping Commercial Intertextuality: HBO's True Blood', *Convergence*, 17(1), pp. 7–17.

Hardy, J. (2013) *Cross-Media Promotion*, New York, NY: Peter Lang.

Hon, A. (2001) *The Guide*, 09.2001. Available: http://web.archive.org/web/20060116100956/www.cloudmakers.org:80/guide/ [Accessed 11.01.2019].

Hon, A. (2012) *Interview with Author*, 26.10.2012, London.

Hoxsey, R. (2005) 'Stranger Than Unfiction', *Print*, 59(4), pp. 102–103.

Irwin, M. J. (2007) 'Q&A with Alternate Reality Games Director Elan Lee', *Wired Magazine*, 15(6). 17.05.2007. Available: https://web.archive.org/web/20130614215450/www.wired.com/gaming/virtualworlds/magazine/15-06/st_arg3 [Accessed 11.01.2019].

Janes, S. (2016) '"You Had to Be There" – ARGs and Multiple Durational Temporalities', in Sara Pesce & Paolo Noto, eds., *The Politics of Ephemeral Digital Media*, London: Routledge, pp. 183–197.

Janes, S. (2017) 'Promotional Alternate Reality Games (ARGs) and the TINAG Philosophy', in Antero Garcia & Greg Niemeyer, eds., *Alternate Reality Games and the Cusp of Digital Gameplay*, London: Bloomsbury, pp. 107–130.

Jenkins, H. (2006) *Convergence Culture: Where Old and New Media Collide*, New York, NY; London: New York University Press.

Jurassic World (2015) dir. Colin Trevorrow.

Kerr, J. (2007) *ARGFest Transcript 04 – Panel 2 – Running an ARG*. Available: https://web.archive.org/web/20070825211534/http://wiki.argfestocon.com:80/index.php?title=2007vt04_Transcription [Accessed 11.01.2019].

Kerrigan, F. (2010) *Film Marketing*, Amsterdam; Boston, MA; London: Elsevier, Butterworth-Heinemann.

Kinder, M. (2002) 'Hot Spots, Avatars and Narrative Fields Forever: Bunuel's Legacy for New Digital Media and Interactive Database Narrative', *Film Quarterly*, 55(4), pp. 2–15.

Koelsch, D. (2011) 'Super 8 Viral Recap and Review', *Movieviral.com*, 16.06.2011. Available: www.movieviral.com/2011/06/16/super-8-viral-recap-and-review/ [Accessed 11.01.2019].

Kyllo, B. (2009) 'ARG Creator's Got Game', *The Globe and Mail*. Available: www.theglobeandmail.com/news/technology/article687821.ece [Accessed 24.06.2009]. No longer available online. Print copy held by author.

Landau, P. (2001) ' "A.I." Promotion', *Adweek*, 42(46).

Lee, E. (2002) *This Is Not a Game: A Discussion of the Creation of the AI Web Experience*, Game Developers Conference, San Jose, CA, 22.03.2002. Available: http://groups.yahoo.com/neo/groups/cloudmakers/files [Accessed 11.01.2019].

Lyczba, F. (2017) 'Hoaxing the Media: 1920s Film Ballyhoo and an Archaeology of Presence', in Sara Pesco & Paolo Noto, eds., *The Politics of Ephemeral Digital Media*, London: Routledge, pp. 110–123.

McCarthy, E. J. (1960) *Basic Marketing: A Managerial Approach*, Homewood, IL: R.D. Irwin.

Mittell, J. (2006) 'Narrative Complexity in Contemporary American Television', *The Velvet Light Trap*, 58, pp. 29–40, Fall.

Mittell, J. (2009) '*Lost* in a Great Story: Evaluation in Narrative Television (and Television Studies)', in Roberta Pearson, ed., *Reading Lost*, London: I. B. Tauris, pp. 119–138.

Murray, J. H. (1997) *Hamlet on the Holodeck: The Future of Narrative in Cyberspace*, New York, NY; London: Free Press.

New York Times. (1938) 'Radio Listeners in Panic, Taking War Drama as Fact', *New York Times*, 31.10.1938.

Panek, E. (2006) 'The Poet and the Detective: Defining the Psychological Puzzle Film', *Film Criticism*, 31(1–2), pp. 62–88.

Powell, H., ed. (2013) *Promotional Culture and Convergence: Markets, Methods, Media* London; New York, NY: Routledge.

Readon, J. (2009) 'Alternative Reality', *Brand Strategy*, (229), pp. 44–45, 02.2009.

Rose, F. (2011) *The Art of Immersion: How the Digital Generation Is Remaking Hollywood, Madison Avenue and the Way We Tell Stories* New York, NY: W. W. Norton & Company.

Ruberg, B. (2006) 'Elan Lee's Alternate Reality', *Gamasutra.com*. Available: www.gamasutra.com/view/feature/130182/elan_lees_alternate_reality.php [Accessed 11.01.2019].

Serazio, M. (2013) *Your Ad Here: The Cool Sell of Guerrilla Marketing*, New York, NY: New York University Press.

Siegel, S. J. (2006) 'Joystiq Interviews Elan Lee of 42 Entertainment', *Joystiq.com*, 14.11.2006. Available: www.engadget.com/2006/11/14/joystiq-interviews-elan-lee-of-42-entertainment [Accessed 11.01.2019].

Simons, J. (2008) 'Complex Narratives', *New Review of Film and Television Studies*, 6(2), pp. 111–126.

Smith, N. (2008) 'Following the Scent', *New Media Age*, pp. 23–24, 09.10.2008.

Staiger, J. (2006) 'Complex Narratives, an Introduction', *Film Criticism*, 31(1–2), pp. 2–172.

Stewart, S. (2012) *Interview with Author*, 10–12.2012, London.

Szulborski, D. (2005) *This Is Not a Game: A Guide to Alternate Reality Gaming*, Seattle, WA: Incunabula.

Telotte, J. P. (2001) 'The Blair Witch Project Project: Film and the Internet', *Film Quarterly*, 54(9), pp. 32–39.

The Blair Witch Project (1999) dir. Daniel Myrick & Eduardo Sánchez.

Unfiction Glossary. 2011. Available: www.unfiction.com/glossary [Accessed 11.01.2019].

Vargo, S. & Lusch, R. (2006) 'Service-Dominant Logic: What It Is, What It Is Not, What It Might Be', in S. Vargo & R. Lusch, eds., *The Service-Dominant Logic of Marketing*, Armonk, NY: M.E. Sharpe.

Walmsley, B. (2018) 'The Death of Arts Marketing: A Paradigm Shift from Consumption to Enrichment', *Arts and the Market*. ISSN 2056-4945 (In Press).

Watson, R. (2001) 'Film with No Advertising, But Everyone Will Know About It', *BBC Newsnight Online*, 30.04.2001. Available: http://news.bbc.co.uk/1/hi/events/newsnight/1312946.stm [Accessed 17.04.2019].

Williams, K. (1979) *Masquerade*, London: Jonathan Cape.

Wilson, G. (2006) 'Transparency and Twist in the Narrative Fiction Film', *The Journal of Aesthetics and Art Criticism*, 64(1), pp. 81–95.

2 ARGs as marketing

With the audience's attention split across multiple digital and social media platforms as well as traditional TV, film, and radio, the need for media companies and their products to be present in as many of those spaces as possible is now taken for granted. The seamless co-ordination and integration of content across platforms is now the challenge. The emergence of promotional ARGs can be viewed in a broader context of 'transmedia storytelling' and 'cross-platform' engagement. From a promotional perspective, transmedia entertainment can be defined as: 'the co-ordinated flow of stories, characters and images that enhance the customer's experience of a brand' (Powell 2013: 10). A related term is 'cross-media marketing', which Hardy defines as 'the promotion of one media service or product through another', specifically the synergistic practice of media firms cross-promoting their 'allied media interests' (2010: 4). Promotional ARGs function as world-builders and story-sellers, yet there is a drive to view these functions as oppositional, or mutually exclusive. Striking a balance between being pieces of narrative storytelling and a driving force for the sale of another product is no simple task.

With these dual roles in mind, this chapter examines the relationship between promotional ARGs, wider campaign materials, and the films they are tasked with marketing. It also examines how each case study engages with a variety of marketing theories and strategies, including affective economics, branding/branded entertainment, commercial sponsorship, and brand communities.

Wider campaign materials

Entry points to all three case studies relied on players noticing something unusual hidden in conventional promotional materials, that is, trailers, posters, official websites. Warner Bros.' official website for *A.I.* was not initially involved in the ARG, but the marketing team later allowed ARG producers to use it to point newcomers towards the game (Puppetmaster FAQ 2001). However, the Microsoft team and Warner Bros. marketing team were distinctly separate entities. This accounts for the way Lee and Stewart describe the game as a genre of storytelling, rather than a piece of marketing. They emphasise that Warner Bros. were supportive of the project, but tend to speak vaguely about its financial success. Lee also recalls PMs did not monitor player demographics, which would have been in the interest of the marketing team (Lee 2002). Given their close relationship, players may have responded negatively if it appeared they were being sold to, so the Microsoft team may have distanced themselves from marketers to maintain that trust.

WhySoSerious worked more closely with other official materials. Increased access to broadband internet connections cemented the use of official websites as rabbit hole locations, and posters or trailers were awarded for solving puzzles. However, all ARG sites were distinctly independent of the initial launch site. Channelling official content to fans in this manner could be viewed as an attempt to control the dissemination of that content, keeping fans happy and dissuading them from finding and leaking content through less desirable channels.

Conversely, the Super 8 ARG returned players to the official site (super8-movie.com) at a later stage in the game to find the Editing Room. Several 'official' channels also connected to the Editing Room as means of unlocking clips (iPhone/iPad app, theatre standees). This breaks with TINAG, as although it provides information supporting the ARG, the Editing Room does not exist in the alternate reality with Josh Minker. The affiliation with the marketing campaign is made clear by the official website, yet if 'this is not a game' then by extension it is also not advertising and should not announce its status as such too loudly.

The Editing Room also seemed separate from scariestthingieversaw.com, and Christiano (2013) confirmed the two were developed in parallel but did not relate to each other. The Rocket Poppetteers thread was run by Watson D/G, who had contact with Project C but did not collaborate with them creatively. Other separate initiatives included the Twitter campaign #Super-8Secret, which gave away tickets to preview screenings across the US. Fans also had the opportunity to design artwork for the cover of a downloadable *Super 8* comic. Finally, a further site was launched by Paramount UK closer to the UK release date. Gonnabemint.com allowed users to browse the contents of a desk belonging to the film's central character, Joe Lamb. It contained ARG references, including Rocket Poppeteers and a toolbox similar to the one in which Josh discovered his father's final note. However, the ARG had been presumed finished for a month before this site was discovered, and it did not revive the Minker narrative.

These numerous access points made it difficult to distinguish ARG content from the wider campaign, and players began to feel the game was being ignored in favour of developing smaller, disconnected viral elements for a wider audience:

> *It would be nice if we common ARG folk could be active players instead of just being fed occasional pictures and blog posts. How about some kind of puzzles or real world quests for us?*
>
> (UF)

> *I fear sometimes they try to invest in other target groups, which could sometimes fail, because addressed people don't care about the movie, and we, who cares, are le*[f]*t out.*
>
> (UF)

Many of these access points were mediated via sites such as Slashfilm and Wired, rather than being hidden online for players to hunt down themselves. Super 8 therefore had more links to other official marketing materials than previous promotional ARGs, but blurred their boundaries in a manner unfamiliar and sometimes frustrating to players.

Paraxtextual positioning

All three ARGs position themselves in a way which is completely different from, if not oppositional to, what Wyatt (1994) calls 'high concept'. This posits a relationship between marketing and films in which the two are stylistically integrated, with films relying on bold, heavily visual marketing, clearly outlining the kind of film viewers should expect. They demonstrate aesthetic and, to varying degrees, narrative integration between film and marketing content. Examples include *Jaws* (Steven Spielberg 1975), *Flashdance* (Adrian Lyne 1983), and *Top Gun* (Tony Scott 1986). In contrast, being puzzle-based, ARGs tend to withhold, rather than explicate, information about the film, challenging audiences to find it themselves. Their dual role as promotion/narrative extension means they serve as new creative content, but that content is restricted by the genres and settings of the films they promote. Promotional ARGs therefore have a more complicated relationship with those films, juggling linear narrative extension, character development, and worldbuilding with varying degrees of success. They are also tasked with supplying a sense of exclusivity – a perspective on the storyworld available solely to privileged players.

The Beast is the least narratively integrated ARG of the three. Set 16 years after the film, *A.I.* provided a context for and supported The Beast, not the other way around. Seeing the film was not essential to completing the game. Both Lee and Stewart read the script and felt the film's sci-fi genre and themes about family could be translated effectively into a game story, but Stewart describes the two as 'very different beasts' in terms of storylines (Cloudmakers 2001). He also states the film was a 'done deal' with the ARG created 'inside that infrastructure', rather than developing in tandem (Cloudmakers 2001). Having discarded the pre-planned game schedule within the first week, it's also hard to say from the texts alone whether links between game and film were always intentional. Characters relevant to *A.I.* did not appear in The Beast until about halfway through, requiring players to be completely involved before any direct intersection with the film occurred. Goodridge described the game as a 'decoy' because neither Jeanine Salla nor Evan Chan featured in the film (Goodridge 2001: 6).

The closest direct link to the film's narrative was the storyline regarding Martin Swinton (played by Jake Thomas), a human child having difficulty coming to terms with the existence of his A.I. 'brother' David (played by Haley Joel Osment). A dark sibling rivalry develops, and disturbing events cause their mother Monica to take David back to the manufacturers, where he will be destroyed. Unable to send him to his demise, Monica instead abandons him in a forest, and David is left to fend for himself as an unauthorised A.I.

The ARG starts with the premise that, 16 years later, Martin still struggles with guilt over his brother's disappearance. He discovers David's creators have been working on further versions of him, along with an A.I. copy of Monica to take care of them. Monica blames Martin for David's disappearance and lures him to an A.I. lab to kill him. Martin outwits her by speaking the activation code causing an A.I. child to feel love for its parents. Internally conflicted by the instruction to love the child she hates, Monica is destroyed.

Even here, the sense of a direct linear extension of the film's narrative is somewhat loose since Martin ceases to be a key character in the film once David has been abandoned. This indirect link suggests the ARG is more involved with Beck's (2004) idea of worldbuilding, creating a more immersive viewing experience. The two complement each other but could be considered stand-alone stories occurring within the same filmic world. What links them are broader themes: the genre of science fiction, family, what it means to be human, and what Stewart describes as a 'novel-style' interpretation of the film's visuals. The film provided stunning depictions of a world where global warming had left New York City submerged and frozen over. The ARG delved further into the science behind this and made it a central narrative feature. It used websites peripheral to the main narrative to flesh out the world of 2142 with creative artwork and detailed articles. All websites in The Beast were designed with distinct visual and writing styles, and Cloudmakers commented on the strong characterisation and sense of atmosphere. The ARG was arguably more successful as a game in its own right than as a piece of marketing – a rare instance of what Gray describes as 'the paratext trumping the film' (2010: 176).

WhySoSerious had a clearer sense of linear extension, occupying a narrative gap between *Batman Begins* and *The Dark Knight*. It was not necessary to see either film to play the game, but the ARG's final act does set up the opening sequence of the film, creating strong narrative continuity. However, events in WhySoSerious contributed not only towards linear extension, but also to a fuller depiction of the world of Gotham. The game picked up a world originating in Frank Miller's graphic novels and continued its existence, inviting players into Gotham's timeline at beginning of the Joker's chaotic campaign. Some events (e.g. stories of corruption in the GDP) were not overly significant in themselves but established an atmosphere of suspicion and mistrust. As citizens of Gotham, players took part in tasks on behalf of the Joker, Harvey Dent, and Gotham Police, allowing them to experience different facets of that world. This was expanded by detailed, convincing websites for other institutions including the press, broadcast media, public transport authorities, and retailers. These websites pushed the narrative forward, but were also designed with TINAG and character development in mind. Gotham's online presence reflected its grittier aesthetics, and visual continuity was established as the Joker vandalised objects in the film in the same style as the jokerised pages in the ARG. Real-world, city-based activities created a greater sense of immersion, as well as highlighting a long-standing theme of the franchise: Gotham City as Every-City. As a reboot this was important not only creatively but commercially. In contrast to the other case studies, WhySoSerious worked within a pre-existing alternate reality which had been significantly reworked. That world needed to be carefully and consistently communicated to keep commercially valuable fan audiences on side.

It had a similar task in managing expectations around old-but-new characters. The Joker underwent considerable transformation, from Jack Nicholson's vengeful lunatic created in a chemical plant accident, to Heath Ledger's anarchic, amoral terrorist with no fixed motivations or clear origins. Similarly, Aaron Eckhart's Harvey Dent is more complex than Tommy Lee Jones' Two-Face, becoming more the tragic hero than the villain. Much of the film focusses on his attempts to put the mob out of business as district attorney. When he does turn villain, Batman accepts this status to ensure Gotham remembers Dent as the hero, concealing the fact that the Joker has corrupted the man Gotham viewed as its saviour. The ARG was key in revealing just enough about these complicated characters to manage expectations. The design of the Joker's pages reflected his maniacal and anarchic nature, crucial to Ledger's characterisation. Two-Face was not explicitly revealed during the ARG, but Dent's personality and politics were clearly outlined and there were allusions to his future identity. Although each of the Joker's events led to the next, they functioned as much to exemplify his desire to destroy Gotham as to progress a narrative. Likewise, Dent's campaign served as much to tell players about his character as to tell the story of the election race. This approach arguably outlined the characters with more immediacy than traditional promotional materials.

In Gray's (2010: 3) terms, WhySoSerious is a paratext that provides a definitive 'lens' through which viewers experience the film. It acts as a filter for meaning and provides a formative encounter with the text. It is, of course, only a proposed reading strategy; it is unlikely, impossible even, that every viewer used this filter in the same way, if at all. Those with no exposure to the marketing campaign may have had different viewing experiences. However, WhySoSerious does demonstrate how a filter can be controlled by producers to encourage a preferred reading, rather than provide opportunities for viewers to create their own.

Super 8's ARG drove players towards the film in a stronger manner, positioning itself as part of the film's linear storyline via the short film in the Editing Room. The identity of Josh's father, mystery of the creature, and role of the Argus cubes could only be solved by seeing the film. This made sense for marketers looking to keep focus on the product, but by this point players had come to expect a more expansive world to explore and inhabit, beyond a backstory for the film.

Coherent worldbuilding came with a different set of challenges for Super 8. Like The Beast, the film preceded the game chronologically and characters from the game did not appear in the film (with the exception of Dr Woodward). However, unlike The Beast's carte blanche of a futuristic 2142, or WhySoSerious' pre-established Gotham City, Super 8 had to work with the film's relatively recent reality of the late 1970s. Nostalgia for that era, its cinema and technologies, is a central theme of the film. It is by no means a documentary-realist portrayal; it is an imagined 1979, a cinephilic vision, coloured heavily by homages to previous Spielberg films. Nevertheless, the filmic reality was positioned much closer to our own.

That the internet did not exist in 1979 is problematic when utilising a storytelling genre rooted in that medium. Characters cannot have blogs or email accounts for players to hack; companies cannot have corporate websites. Building a convincing alternate reality based in the past may therefore necessitate forfeiting a convincing TINAG aesthetic. Super 8 partially overcame this by setting the ARG storyline in the present, with Josh investigating his father's past. Unfortunately, the film's nostalgic recreation of the late '70s was sometimes more interesting than the present-day setting of the ARG. Design elements also felt inconsistent in places. Josh Minker's blog, although designed to look amateur, used formats and fonts which appeared *too* dated. Revalistic.com, apparently a conspiracy theory site, was incredibly sparse, but a brief look at other 'conspiracy' sites establishes them as visually cluttered.[1] Revalistic.com became primarily a method of undercover communication between Josh and Sarah, but this felt like a simple platform for handing out narrative information to players, rather than something designed to reflect either the characters or the wider game universe.

Compared to the plethora of carefully constructed sites in WhySoSerious and The Beast, Super 8 made regular use of very few. There was a lack of peripheral content to expand the game world or developed characterisation rather than simply further the narrative. This meant players seeking to push further into that world became frustrated when they found nothing more. Information like Josh Minker's interest in rare fish appeared to function more as a red herring (pun intended?) than as character development. Josh's world was too disconnected from film protagonist Joe Lamb's for it to feel like the ARG was a coherent expansion of a *Super 8* universe. The only in-game reference to Joe was his name scratched on the tin in which Josh found the final message from his father. How it got there was never established, and the connection never fully explained.[2]

There is a distinct mismatch here between the playful, game-like pleasures of an ARG and the more bounded experience of the film it seeks to sell. This can be viewed as 'added value' for the more established medium, or a jarring rift, in which case the game becomes more engaging than the film, or highlights the shortcomings of both. Either way, the sense of linear narrative extension in Super 8 was not matched by the kind of worldbuilding players had come to expect from an ARG. Super 8's strong connection with the wider marketing campaign and loose connection to the world of the film risked falling into Gray's (2010: 209–210) category of 'mere marketing', a status which could disappoint players who signed up for deeper narrative engagement.

However, all three ARGs provided a strong sense of exclusivity, offering players prior knowledge of characters and storylines which non-players could not access. The Beast provided this in a more general manner, outlining, for example, A.I. politics, which are important in the film but not detailed as precisely. WhySoSerious made specific references to minor characters in the film. Gotham Tonight host Mike Engel is held hostage by the Joker, and players witness the death of Brian Douglass, leader of the Citizens for Batman forum. These less high-profile characters were familiar to players, allowing them to highlight their membership of this exclusive ARG club by spotting references and demonstrating their cultural capital.

Super 8 similarly allows viewers to spot references to the ARG. Charles has a Rocket Poppeteers poster on his bedroom wall, and one of Joe's t-shirts features a Captain Coop logo. When the children discover Dr Woodward's research, they also find the video from the Editing Room. However, the film went no further than confirming what players already knew. It rewarded their knowledge by affirming it, but did not build on it. Unlike WhySoSerious, which had to work with viewers' existing prior knowledge, Super 8 could provide that knowledge for them beforehand to deploy in the film. The ARG effectively constructed a fan experience for them. Charles' and Joe's rooms were a mass of classic movie posters, models, books, and comics; a heavily detailed mise-en-scène which could be fruitfully picked over if one took the time. This encouraged an affective mode of reception in line with theories of affective economics.

Affective economics and fanification

All three ARGs tap into Jenkins' theory of affective economics (2006: 61). Affect (verb) is defined as 'to produce an effect upon', but also has emotional significance: 'to act upon (as a person or a person's mind or feelings) so as to produce a response' (Merriam-Webster Online Dictionary 2014). In marketing, affect is ultimately intended to provoke a purchasing decision, but Jenkins (2006) posits an alternative theory of 'affective economics'. This 'seeks to understand the emotional underpinnings of consumer decision-making as a driving force behind viewing and purchasing decisions' (2006: 61–62). Once they understand those emotional attachments, marketers can attempt to shape them, getting people emotionally involved with brands or products. Buzzwords include 'emotional capital' and 'lovemarks' as opposed to brands (Jenkins 2006: 69–70).

This is not necessarily a new approach. Grainge notes a shift in the 1950s from 'instrumental to emotional advertising' whereby the 'ubiquity and significance of promotional communication [is] based not on what customers know about a product but on how they are made to feel and identify as consuming subjects' (2007: 23). Brands are therefore less interested in communicating product information and more interested in how they make consumers feel; what emotions, aspirations, or ideals they communicate. Affective economics positions the consumer as not only the receptor of those messages, but as a reciprocal investor, actively bringing those emotions to bear upon the brand which then dictates their purchasing decisions. The interactive and communal nature of an ARG can allow producers to encourage and develop this affective relationship in ways other media cannot.

Hills (2002: xiii) suggests a focus on the personal, emotional, and subjective experience of fandom means the notion of power in the consumer/producer relationship is less important. However, an ARG creates and sells an emotional, subjective experience back to fans. In this situation, discussions about the personal and subjective nature of fandom no longer circumvent questions of power or control – they become central to that debate. Jenkins develops this argument by claiming affective economics gives consumers more control over media products (2006: 63). Whether the emotional attachment created by ARGs provides this is debatable, as is the ensuing question of whether players desire higher levels of control. They may even be willing to relinquish control, if they feel they have received an entertaining game experience in return. Chapter 3 investigates these claims further.

The characters, companies, and storylines in The Beast may have served to explicate the world of the film to the extent that players were more emotionally invested in it. Interacting with this world (particularly with characters) heightens this sense of personal involvement, as does the close relationship with PMs. It was even suggested that the ARG offered 'an emotional involvement that the film cannot hope to match' (Gallagher 2001). This might appear to be a failure on the part of the game to transfer these feelings to the film, but the mere association of the two suggests a desire to achieve this connection. The assumption is that the more time the user spends participating, the stronger the emotional bond (Powell 2013: 12). Indeed, 80% of surveyed players agreed a good ARG left them more emotionally invested in the film it was promoting, and 90% said it made them more likely to see the film.

This kind of affective engagement is often associated with fan audiences. In addition, the detail-oriented nature of ARGs encourages mainstream Hollywood audiences to engage in 'forensic fandom' (Mittell 2009). As Powell notes, 'The capacity to transform users into fans who will seek out and share all further opportunities to acquire both the tangible and intangible elements of any media product becomes a highly profitable marketing tool' (2013: 10). Nikunen (2007) describes this as 'fanification', and the Unfiction forum attests to this 'forensic' mode of engagement, full of passionate discussion about every element of the game.

However, it is debatable whether ARGs transform casual consumers into brand evangelists. Surveyed players are self-selecting in that they are more active members of the player community, and they are emphatically in the minority. Not every player engages in enough depth for that affective investment to happen, and there is no guarantee their enthusiasm will filter down to the larger lurker audience. Designers were tasked with creating experiences that appealed to all players, from lurkers to hardcore code-crackers, but this continued to prove challenging. As the genre developed it became clear ARGs were more effective for properties with existing dedicated fanbases who had already made those emotional investments, such as *The Dark Knight* or *Tron: Legacy* (Walden 2016).

Branding and brand ownership

A promotional ARG is ultimately part of a wider branding strategy for the film or franchise. However, as Grainge and Johnson (2015) note, positioning films-as-brands is complex since they are often both brands themselves and components of larger franchises. ARGs fit into a pattern whereby marketing and promotion is a process of positioning the film to audiences over months or years, rather than weeks before theatrical release. Their immersive nature and relatively lengthy durations invite audiences to submerge themselves in the film world/brand.

Grainge's (2007) concept of 'total entertainment' is useful here. It explains the 'branding' of Hollywood films in a manner which is appropriately industry-specific, involving both aesthetic and industrial logics. In this context, ARGs form part of the 'inhabitable' universe which media conglomerates seek to create around a film, for example, players are invited to become 'citizens of Gotham'. Agency within that world, particularly the potential for players to affect the outcome of a narrative, may provide an understanding of the brand not purely shaped by marketers, but by players' lived experiences of the game and the direction in which they and the community take it. The effect of this fannish engagement is a strong sense of empowerment and ownership. The player community frequently distinguishes between what marketing content is 'for us' and what is for a wider, uninitiated audience. Jenkins (2006) suggests this emotional connection to the brand, and the collaborative nature of the game, is a basis for increased consumer power. The level of interactivity and participation required even prompted one *Businessweek* article to proclaim ARGs as 'Brand Democracy' (Kiley 2005). It suggests ARGs allow consumers, not marketers, to determine how brands are communicated.

Conversely, Grainge (2007) argues the industrial principle behind 'total entertainment' is one of near total control for conglomerates. Viewers are seemingly invited to participate with the brand, but only in ways which do not threaten the media conglomerate's IP. Players create narratives with content fed to them by PMs but are rarely invited to create their own, because this could adversely affect the overall brand message. Indeed, a senior vice president of digital marketing at Universal confirms this concern with reference to Cloverfield's ARG: 'We like our materials to always be on message. There's always a risk if fans are discovering that [message] on their own' (Brodesser-Akner 2007). ARGs also offer exclusive trailers or stills as rewards for completing tasks. It could be argued that measured release of this material is designed to deter consumers from searching for it elsewhere, using players as an influential marketing channel through which producers can still control their content. WhySoSerious allowed players to participate in Nolan's vision of Gotham, but it did not allow them to construct it. This is not to diminish the creative and emotional significance of that participation, but one might question how 'democratic' such strategies are and whether consumers really desire that kind of relationship with media brands.

Branded content/branded entertainment

ARGs also fit the relatively new category of 'branded content' or 'branded entertainment'. The development of both terms reflects an increasing slippage between strictly promotional content and editorial or entertainment content. Definitions have been attempted from an industry perspective, but a firm agreement is hard to come by. A 2016 report commissioned by the Branded Content Marketing Association describes it as:

> . . . any output fully/partly funded or at least endorsed by the legal owner of the brand which promotes the owner's brand values, and makes audiences choose to engage with the brand based on a pull logic due to its entertainment, information and/or education value.
>
> (Asmussen et al. 2016)

The Branded Content Research Network (2016) expands on this by noting:

> Some of this is brands' 'owned' media content (e.g. content published on the brand's own website, social media sites, YouTube channel etc.) and the manner of publication makes clear that the communication is paid for and controlled by the brand. However, much branded content is material that appears as editorial content in third-party publications, sites or online spaces that are nominally independent of the brand.[3]

This is problematic in terms of user trust and media integrity, as it becomes difficult to distinguish between editorial and sponsored content, particularly in online publications (Goodman 2006; Hardy 2017a, 2017b). This practice reflects industry concerns that audiences are becoming adept at dodging online advertising. Embedding promotional material into entertainment content is an effective way to get users to engage with marketing messages without necessarily realising they have done so. Ongoing debates highlight the importance of media literacy in the contemporary transmedia landscape, not only in terms of identifying promotional intent where it is obscured (West & McAllister 2013: 7), but also in tackling 'fake news' and encouraging more critical understandings of media bias (Mihailidis & Viotty 2017; Lee 2018). This immediately calls to mind the TINAG philosophy governing ARGs. If This Is Not A Game, then This Is Not A Marketing Campaign either, and the games should not announce themselves as such. In earlier ARGs, the risk of hoaxing was considered more carefully as audiences got used to a game aesthetic that strived to look as much like real life as possible (Dena 2007, 2008a). However, in games promoting films or TV series this tended to be less of a risk. Super 8's integration with 'officially' branded Paramount content was very clear indeed, which risked breaking TINAG, but players were generally amenable to this in the context of promotional games:

> *When it's based on a movie/TV show, we know where it's coming from,*
> *and corporations have to protect their copyright. So the presence of*
> *branding isn't so bad.*

(UF)[4]

In fact, ARGs that do not subtly indicate their association with brands from the outset risk alienating players altogether, jeopardising the mutual trust that enables them to run. Whether content is in/out of game, or is more/less promotional in its purpose, is analysed at length in forums. This indicates a highly media-literate audience that enjoys playing with the slippage between the boundaries of reality/fiction, promotion/content in complex ways. As McGonigal (2007) notes, half the joy of playing is 'performing' TINAG – performing the suspension of disbelief and choosing to engage/disengage with it in different ways throughout. Promotional ARGs may demonstrate more playful, less deceptive ways of 'doing' branded content.

The blurring of these boundaries in screen industries has prompted changes in organisational structures and working practices to the extent that Grainge and Johnson argue for the emergence of a 'promotional screen industries' sector. They view it not as 'a clearly defined sector, but a fluid, fast-moving site of industrial collaboration and competition, with promotional intermediaries from different fields moving into each other's territories' (Grainge & Johnson 2015: 8). They call for the recognition of promotional screen production as a creative and professional discipline, which requires 'stepping beyond critical dualisms that set creativity against marketing as the default of promotional analysis' (2015: 4).

ARGs support this, emerging at a point where film, television, and advertising industries were developing a 'recognition of such work *as* creative content' (Grainge & Johnson 2015: 6). Askwith's definition of them as 'collision of traditional promotional marketing and new immersive narrative content' (2006: 16) puts them squarely in this camp, and WhySoSerious picked up several industry awards indicating this level of recognition. The

Beast and Super 8 involved collaborations between science fiction novelists, game designers, film directors, and video content editors/producers, amongst other cross-sector partnerships. Yet, accounts from ARG designers (particularly in the early 2000s) still suggested a division between those who considered the games as creative storytelling and those who prioritised their promotional role, conceptualising their value differently.

In 2014, former 42 Entertainment PM Steve Peters launched a crowd-funding campaign for the transmedia experience Project Alibi. The language on the Indiegogo page suggests this feeling persists among transmedia designers: 'This is a project we've been eager to bring to you for a quite some time, without the shackles of clients or serving someone else's story.'[5] Grainge and Johnson's work reinforces this sense that 'promotional screen work is still often cast low within the hierarchies of artistic value . . . serving instrumental needs of marketing and commerce' (2015: 78). Promotional work is still viewed and experienced as something which restricts creative control and autonomy. ARGs demonstrate that this tension is still present and unresolved in a continuously changing and evolving promotional content industry. However, the desire of ARG designers to reclaim that creative control is indicative of Grainge and Johnson's (2015) assertions that these games, amongst other promotional media, are indeed the product of creative and artistic labour and are slowly being recognised as such.

Brand community

ARGs require the formation of a distinct player community, which appears to make them relevant to notions of 'brand community' (Muniz & O'Guinn 2001) or 'communities of consumption' (Kozinets 1999). Players have varying motivations for signing up to ARGs, but in promotional games there are often multiple communities of interest at work. Fan communities play a significant role, whether they are fans of the film, franchise, actors, or directors, making this relationship more complex.

Muniz and O'Guinn define a brand community as

> a specialised, non-geographically bound community, based on a structured set of social relationships among admirers of a brand . . . at its centre is a branded good or service . . . it is marked by a shared consciousness, rituals and traditions, and a sense of moral responsibility. Each of these qualities is, however, situated within a commercial and mass mediated ethos, and has its own particular expression.
>
> (2001: 412)

Brand communities embrace rather than reject the ideology of commercial culture. They see brand meanings as socially and subjectively negotiated, 'rather than delivered unaltered and in toto from context to context, consumer to consumer' (Muniz & O'Guinn 2001: 414). They are not naïve consumers but are conscious of the commercial context of their communities and act with self-awareness. Instead of being lost to the alienation and atomisation of postmodernity, the community is alive and well, existing comfortably within consumer culture.

McAlexander et al. (2002) expand these ideas, suggesting that, as an extension of relationship marketing, customer experience is at the centre of brand community. Both studies evidence how brand communities contribute to increased personal investment in brands, repurchase rates, and improved brand reputation. McAlexander et al. note the lengths to which Jeep marketers go to maintain good relationships with consumers, ranging from barbeques to weekend-long 'brandfests' (2002: 42). Both studies also acknowledge the problems posed by brand communities. They may reject or oppose brand messages, damaging the brand's overall perception. Intense hierarchies and desires to maintain exclusivity may also be problematic for brands wishing to expand, causing tension between the needs of the producer and the desires of the consumer.

This definition has at its centre 'a branded good or service', and it is the appreciation of this brand which binds the non-geographically linked community (Muniz & O'Guinn 2001: 412). Promotional ARGs may not necessarily create communities whose central concern is the promoted film. They may be interested in ARGs more generally, moving between games regardless of whether they are promotional. Dena (2008b) suggests lurkers interact more with player-produced content (forums, game analysis, game summaries, etc.) than PM-produced content, further distancing them from the film. Kozinets' 'communities of consumption' (1999) are equally difficult to apply to ARG communities. The shared consumption activity could be defined as the playing of ARGs, rather than moviegoing, which the ARG is presumably meant to encourage. If the aim is to create a community around the film-as-brand, there is always a risk the ARG will create a community whose focus is not the film, but the game itself, thus defeating its promotional purpose.

However, Jeremy Reynolds alludes to the role of ARGs in building brand communities when he says,

> As marketing tools, ARGs are excellent because they not only require extended exposure to the advertised product, but they encourage participants to build an authentic group culture that is interwoven with brand communication.
>
> (cited in IGDA 2006)

Emotional investment in both ARG and film is also strengthened by interactions amongst players, creating social bonds and associating personal relationships with that gaming experience. This resonates with both affective economics and brand communities. Whether or not the games represent an active attempt to construct brand communities is less clear, as discussed further in Chapter 3.

Conclusion

Due to its positioning as transmedia narrative content which blurs the lines between fiction and reality, the marketing function of a promotional ARG may not always be immediately clear. Each of the case studies engages differently with wider campaign materials, not always clearly situating itself as part of a cross-media campaign or aligning itself clearly with the media conglomerate which owns the IP it is promoting. This is partly due to differing production contexts, ranging from the experimental Beast to the more tightly commercially controlled WhySoSerious and the multi-agency approach of Super 8. This context similarly impacts the paratextual positioning of each ARG, with each game being variously narratively and/or visually integrated with their respective films. All three examples do, however, demonstrate paratexts which seek to frame the experience of the film itself in a particular manner, and to attempt a form of 'fanification' of audiences. They all provide a sense of exclusivity for players and encourage an affective, fan-like mode of reception.

This allows marketers to take advantage of affective economics, encouraging emotional investments in the game which ideally transfer to the product being marketed. They might also be viewed as an attempt to create (and partially control) the activities of a 'brand community' around the promoted media product. Whether or not ARGs turn casual viewers into brand evangelists is debatable, as is the notion that this kind of emotional investment empowers audiences to influence the media content they want from producers. Promotional ARGs appear to reflect a more open and co-operative stance from media conglomerates in relation to fan audiences, offering them a sense of co-ownership of the content in which they are invested. Yet, to describe them as a form of 'brand democracy' seems a stretch of some optimism. The next chapter looks more closely at notions of 'meaningful' participation in promotional ARGs, whether this is possible in a promotional context, and what kinds of empowerment, if any, they might offer consumers.

Notes

1 For examples, see http://www.abovetopsecret.com/ or http://www.theinsider.org/ [Accessed 05.07.2019].
2 It is possible Woodward took the tin from Joe during a lesson, as the protagonists mention his tendency to confiscate items. However, this is speculative and never confirmed in the game or film.
3 See also Hardy 2018.
4 WhySoSerious involved prominent sponsors, including Domino's, Nokia, and Comcast. The role and impact of in-game branding and sponsorship is a wide area of research, from effectiveness to regulation (Nelson et al. 2004; Grossman 2005; Grimes 2008; Lewis & Porter 2010). The Lost Experience saw complaints from players about poorly integrated sponsorship breaking TINAG (Askwith 2007), and Mittell (2006) notes it 'irritated' many players because it was integrated in a 'tacky and superfluous' way without 'significant payoff'. Although fascinating, it is not within the scope of this book to fully examine the role of these additional advertising strategies embedded in promotional ARGs.
5 www.indiegogo.com/projects/project-alibi-a-multi-platform-ghost-story#/

References

Askwith, I. (2006) *This Is Not (Just) an Advertisement: Understanding Alternate Reality Games*, MIT Convergence Culture Consortium White Paper. Available: http://convergenceculture.org/research/c3_not_just_an_ad.pdf [Accessed 11.01.2019].
Askwith, I. (2007) *Deconstructing the Lost Experience: In-Depth Analysis of an ARG*, MIT Convergence Culture Consortium White Paper. Available: http://convergenceculture.org/resources/2006/12/deconstructing_the_lost_experi.php [Accessed 11.01.2019].
Asmussen, B., et al. (2016) *Defining Branded Content for the Digital Age. The Industry Experts' Views on Branded Content as a New Marketing Communications Concept.* Available: www.thebcma.info/wp-content/uploads/2016/07/BCMA-Research-Report_FINAL.pdf [Accessed 15.01.2019].
Beck, J. (2004) 'Concept of Narrative: An Analysis of Requiem for a Dream (.com) and Donnie Darko (.com)', *Convergence: The International Journal of Research into New Media Technologies*, 10(3), pp. 55–82.
Branded Content Research Network. (2016) Available: www.brandedcontentresearchnetwork.org/.
Brodesser-Akner, C. (2007) 'Only Gumshoes Can See This Movie', *Advertising Age*, 78(28), pp. 4–36.
Christiano, J. (2013) *Email Interview with Author*, 06.03.2013.
Cloudmakers. (2001) *Post-Game Puppetmaster Chat*, 31.07.2001. Available: http://groups.yahoo.com/neo/groups/cloudmakers/files [Accessed 11.01.2019].
Dena, C. (2007) *Why ARGs Aren't Hoaxes*, 10.11.2007. Available: www.christydena.com/online-essays/why-args-arent-hoaxes/ [Accessed 18.04.2019].
Dena, C. (2008a) *Anti Hoaxing Strategies and the TINAG Fallacy.* Available: www.christydena.com/2008/01/anti-hoaxing-strategies-and-the-tinag-fallacy/ [Accessed 17.01.2019].

Dena, C. (2008b) *Online Augmentation to 'Emerging Participatory Culture Practices: Player-Created Tiers in Alternate Reality Games'*, 22.01.2008. Available: www. christydena.com/research/Convergence2008/TieringandARGs.html [Accessed 11. 03.2019].

Gallagher, D. F. (2001) 'Some Prefer Online "A.I." Tie-In to the Movie', *The New York Times*, 09.07.2001. Available: www.nytimes.com/2001/07/09/technology/ 09GAME.html [Accessed 05.01.2019].

Goodman, E. (2006) 'Stealth Marketing and Editorial Integrity', *Texas Law Review*, 85, pp. 83–152.

Goodridge, M. (2001) 'Spielberg's AI Turns on Media Machine', *Screen International*, (1313), p. 6.

Grimes, S. (2008) 'Kids' Ad Play: Regulating Children's' Advergames in the Converging Media Context', *International Journal of Communications Law & Policy*, 161, Winter.

Grossman, S. (2005) 'Grant Theft Oreo: The Constitutionality of Advergaming Regulation', *Yale Law Journal*, 116(1).

Grainge, P. (2007) *Brand Hollywood: Selling Entertainment in a Global Media Age*, London: Routledge.

Grainge, P. & Johnson, C. (2015) *Promotional Screen Industries*, London: Routledge.

Gray, J. (2010) *Show Sold Separately: Promos, Spoilers, and Other Media Paratexts*, New York, NY: New York University Press.

Hardy, J. (2010) *Cross-Media Promotion*, New York, NY: Peter Lang.

Hardy, J. (2017a) 'Commentary: Branded Content and Media-Marketing Convergence', *The Political Economy of Communication*, 5(1), pp. 81–87.

Hardy, J. (2017b) 'Sponsored Content Is Compromising Media Integrity', *open Democracy*, 12.04.2017. Available: www.opendemocracy.net/jonathan-hardy/spon sored-content-is-blurring-line-between-advertising-and-editorial [Accessed 17. 01.2019].

Hardy, J. (2018) 'Chapter 7 - Branded content Media and marketing integration' in Hardy, J., Powell, H. MacRury, I. eds. *The Advertising Handbook, Fourth Edition*, London: Routledge pp. 102–122.

Hills, M. (2002) *Fan Cultures*, London; New York, NY: Routledge.

IGDA ARG SIG. (2006) *Alternate Reality Games SIG/Whitepaper International Games Developers Association*. Available: www.christydena.com/wp-content/ uploads/2007/11/igda-alternaterealitygames-whitepaper-2006.pdf.

Jenkins, H. (2006) *Convergence Culture: Where Old and New Media Collide*, New York, NY.; London: New York University Press.

Kiley, D. (2005) 'Advertising of, by, and for the People', *BusinessWeek*, (3944), pp. 63–64.

Kozinets, R. (1999) 'E-Tribalized Marketing? The Strategic Implications of Virtual Communities of Consumption', *European Management Journal*, 17(3), pp. 252–264.

Lee, E. (2002) *This Is Not a Game: A Discussion of the Creation of the AI Web Experience*, Game Developers Conference, San Jose, CA., 22.03.2002. Available: http://groups.yahoo.com/neo/groups/cloudmakers/files [Accessed 11.01.2019].

Lee, N. (2018) 'Fake News, Phishing, and Fraud: A Call for Research on Digital Media Literacy Education Beyond the Classroom', *Communication Education*, 67(4), pp. 460–466.

Lewis, B. & Porter, L. (2010) 'In-Game Advertising Effects', *Journal of Interactive Advertising*, 10(2), pp. 46–60.

McAlexander, J., Schouten, J. & Koenig, H. (2002) 'Building Brand Community', *The Journal of Marketing*, 66(1), pp. 38–54.

McGonigal, J. (2007) 'The Puppetmaster Problem: Design for Real World, Mission Based Gaming', in P. Harrigan & N. Wardrip-Fruin, eds., *Second Person: Role Playing and Story in Games and Playable Media*, Cambridge, MA; London: MIT Press.

Mihailidis, P. & Viotty, S. (2017) 'Spreadable Spectacle in Digital Culture: Civic Expression, Fake News, and the Role of Media Literacies in "Post-Fact" Society', *American Behavioral Scientist*, 61(4), pp. 441–454.

Mittell, J. (2006) 'Lost in an Alternate Reality', *Flow*, 4(7). Available: http://flowtv.org/2006/06/lost-in-an-alternate-reality/.

Mittell, J. (2009) '*Lost* in a Great Story: Evaluation in Narrative Television (and Television Studies)', in Roberta Pearson, ed., *Reading Lost*, London: I. B. Tauris, pp. 119–138.

Muniz, A. & O'Guinn, T. (2001) 'Brand Community', *Journal of Consumer Research*, 27(4), pp. 412–432.

Nelson, M. R. et al. (2004) 'Advertainment or Adcreep Game Players' Attitudes Toward Advertising and Product Placements in Computer Games', *Journal of Interactive Advertising*, 5(1), pp. 3–21.

Nikunen, K. (2007) 'The Intermedial Practices of Fandom', *Nordicom Review*, 28(2), pp. 111–128.

Powell, H., ed. (2013) *Promotional Culture and Convergence: Markets, Methods, Media*, London; New York, NY: Routledge.

Puppetmaster FAQ. (2001) Available: http://web.archive.org/web/20020810185009/http://familiasalla-es.cloudmakers.org:80/credits/note/faq.html [Accessed 11.01.2019].

Walden, K. (2016) 'Nostalgia for the Future: How TRON Legacy's Paratextual Campaign Rebooted the Franchise', in Sara Pesce & Paolo Noto, eds., *The Politics of Ephemeral Digital Media*, London: Routledge, pp. 95–109.

West, E. & McAllister, P. (2013) *The Routledge Companion to Advertising and Promotional Culture*, New York, NY: Routledge.

Wyatt, J. (1994) *High Concept: Movies and Marketing in Hollywood*, Austin, TX: University of Texas Press.

3 The promise of participation

McKee (2013: 761) argues that scholars continue to perceive 'power' in media as 'a zero-sum game . . . one agent must have more power'. Commentators tend to fall into optimistic/pessimistic camps, despite acknowledging the complexity of these relationships (2013: 761). Promotional ARGs challenge this perception, since power is constantly negotiated in a genre where producers and consumers respond to each other in real time. The two exist in constant dialogue and are mutually dependent on each other for the game to work. If either side pulls too hard on the strings, the game collapses. However, as complex ARGs are replaced by more carefully controlled virals, media companies appear to be avoiding this kind of relationship, preferring to more heavily dictate how players interact with promotional content.

McKee further notes a propensity to discuss power as a singular entity, when debates historically refer to multiple forms of media power, for example, economic, institutional, or purchasing power (2013: 762). 'Productive' or 'creative' audiences are still privileged as 'empowered' because they are deemed to have an element of control over content and meaning creation. This privileges the power of production over reception when it comes to meaning creation, despite work from Hall's *Encoding/Decoding* (1973) to Jenkins' *Textual Poachers* (1992) which makes clear the importance of reception in that process. Hills (2002) similarly identifies a moral dualism in perceptions of fan communities. The 'good' fan is productive, whereas the 'bad' fan practices a more passive form of fandom (2002: 30).

This is reflected in scholarship on promotional ARGs, focussing on content control as the primary mode of empowerment. Producers also emphasise narrative agency as a key appeal for the games. However, it could be argued that ARGs simply offer players an illusion of textual ownership. The games are increasingly tightly controlled by PMs who in turn are restricted in the kind of agency they can offer by their corporate clients. In some ways that kind of agency was never available at all. Players cannot affect the content of the promoted film; any influence they have exists only within the ARG, the narrative of which is ultimately designed by PMs. Even if it is somewhat shaped by real-time player activity, the balance of power tips towards producers. To describe this as empowerment is somewhat disingenuous. However, this focus on an idealistic and potentially impossible form of consumer empowerment (i.e. control of textual production) risks losing sight of other forms of meaning-making happening on more individual or social levels through participation in promotional ARGs. This chapter examines this primarily from a player perspective, considering their motivations and expectations around 'meaningful' participation, including, but not confined to, narrative control. Players identify strong affective connections with the game content, PMs, and the player community, through which we can consider the potential for a different kind of consumer empowerment. Understanding this requires viewing consumer practices in the same way Hills (2002: 35) demands we look at fan practices – as 'lived experience'. What are players doing with these games, and what meanings and values can they derive from them that might afford them a sense of empowerment?

Meaningful participation: puzzles and live events

Several ARG components could be described as 'interactive' or involving 'audience engagement'. However, this does not mean they are all 'meaningful' to players. Puzzles make an ARG a game, and they necessarily require participation. The Beast had routine online puzzles such as guessing the password for Martin Swinton's diary, which was based on lines in Shakespeare's plays. Others required technical knowledge like HTML, binary code, and hackerspeak. Both WhySoSerious and Super 8 used similar routine puzzles, and WhySoSerious included word puzzles and Flash games. The Beast often required more obscure knowledge, including enigma codes, lute tablature, chemistry, biology, and Japanese sword making. Unfortunately, as Harry Knowles commented, 'It scared a lot of people off because they felt it was just too involving' (Knowles cited in Gallagher 2001). Possibly in response, WhySoSerious and Super 8 rarely required such expertise. Where it was demonstrated by players in Super 8, it went unrewarded. For example, when a sound file appeared on scariestthingieversaw.com, players recorded the notes and frequencies of each tone to establish a pattern. The tones corresponded to the golden ratio,[1] but its relevance was never confirmed. As pieces of marketing, ARGs must provide accessible interactions for both casual and dedicated players. The differences in puzzle design between The Beast and Super 8 suggests this balance has not yet been struck. However, if puzzles become less challenging, this form of interaction may become less meaningful for those looking for a tougher nut to crack.

All online puzzles required some form of collaboration and knowledge sharing, whether due to difficulty, esoteric knowledge, or design of the competition, for example, clues picked up by Joker Phone owners had to be collated and passed to online players to unlock a website. However, the strongest example of collaborative puzzle solving was in offline games, such as the Anti-Robot Militia (ARM) rallies during The Beast. After becoming members of ARM, players received invitations to meetings in bars and restaurants in Chicago, LA, and New York on 6 May 2001. Roughly 40 players attended the New York events, 20 in LA, and 12 in Chicago. They received a leaflet with puzzles leading to three new websites requiring information from each rally, necessitating online communication between cities and across time zones. Levels of mobile internet connectivity at the time would have made this challenging. It took TINAG further than the creation of realistic websites or characters, truly merging the real world and the game world, and was received enthusiastically by players:

> *I just want to say that the rally night was amazing fun and it just boggles my mind how elaborate this game is.*

> (CM)

42 Entertainment went on to set a precedent during Year Zero and ilovebees, leaving high expectations for large-scale live events in WhySoSerious. Rather than being anomalies, such events were central to WhySoSerious, again requiring co-operation between online and ground teams. One event required on-site players to crack the code for an online safe, which directed them to a cinema, where they saw an exclusive new trailer. One member was then given a digital copy to share with the community online. These interactions were also acknowledged within the game world. The Gotham Times reported on scavenger hunts, using photos and names of participants. These events were similarly praised, although players from smaller towns or outside the US were unhappy about their lack of access.

Super 8 had no comparable live events, but this did not stop some players considering the possibility of clues being hidden in an abandoned hospital found on a map provided by a character:

> *I'm almost crazy enough to make the 18 hour drive there and look for something.*

> (UF)

> *I think the email from the curator has essentially confirmed nothing within the building, and the likelihood of hiding something in the area is low (though if someone wanted to check, fantastic).*

> (UF)

The length of this debate suggested an expectation of and desire for real-world events. Online games tended to be aimed at those with more specific 'techie' skills whereas live events tapped into a maturing experience economy and offered a clearer sense of co-operation (Gilmore & Pine 1998). Collaboration is one of the genre's defining features and key to the kind of empowerment Jenkins (2006) envisages for consumers as a collective. However, in the drive to make promotional games more accessible to wider audiences, some of this collaborative work is lost. WhySoSerious was based around co-operative events and communication but did not require the sharing of specific prior knowledge in the same way as The Beast. Elements of Super 8 demanded collaborative work, such as collecting frames through the Editing Room to reveal the full reel. Rocket Poppeteer mini-games divided the community into teams but awarded much-coveted Argus cubes to individuals with high scores, diluting the co-operative nature of the ARG. This competitive play drove players' focus away from PMs and inwards towards the community and their activities. This left less room for conflict to develop between players and PMs, but also facilitated a more distanced relationship.

Furthermore, player communities developed their own hierarchies and competitive relationships, making Jenkins' (2006) knowledge communities less cohesive than they first appear. Hon (2001) estimates '60–80% of all puzzles were solved by the same dozen or so hard-core players'. Others offered speculation, and the odd puzzle was solved by a newcomer. However, Hon (2001) suggests this did not prevent casual players from feeling part of the team. 'When you're a member of the Cloudmakers, and you've made a few speculative posts and suggestions about puzzles you feel like you're contributing and that you're making a difference, even if you're not'. This may not be universally reflected in player testimony, but it is important to acknowledge that the co-operative play so often attributed to ARGs may not always translate into player practice. Competitive play and internal hierarchies are arguably unavoidable but might serve to undermine player empowerment if it is predicated on them functioning as a collective knowledge community.

More broadly, terms like 'interactive', 'engagement', and 'participation' have shifted in meaning. Before broadband connections became commonplace for consumers, ARGs were capitalising on the possibilities surrounding a new connective medium, working with small numbers of early adopters. The prevalence of high-speed connections and social media networks means we now take these kinds of resources for granted, and the impetus is to develop something a larger internet-dwelling audience can enjoy.

In addition, media companies started to question how much they wanted consumers to 'participate' in their brand. By the time Super 8 launched its ARG, engagement could mean as little as liking a Facebook page or retweeting a promotional message. This came with the added benefits of measurable metrics and free amplification of the marketing message, but reduced interaction to the single click required to follow through a banner ad. This did not sit well with experienced players looking for challenging puzzles and events. However, it offered marketers more control and made games easier to measure and monitor quantifiably, while still offering the sense that players had 'participated', albeit minimally. This kind of interactivity is therefore difficult to describe as 'meaningful' in comparison to other elements of a promotional ARG.

Meaningful participation: narrative control

In contrast, the potential for players to assume the role of storyteller was a highly meaningful mode of participation, almost as central to the definition of the genre as puzzles: 'An ARG is a story or a journey . . . driven by an online community whose interaction and experience determines the journey and often the ending' (Smith 2008: 23–24). Nearly 70% of survey respondents agreed 'the ability to affect the outcome of an ARG is one of the genre's main attractions'. Discussions on Unfiction support this:

> *The idea that a player can affect the narrative is not a new one, but ARGs implement it as a more central aspect.*
>
> (UF)

Since there was no precedent for The Beast, players spent a lot of time working out what they could and could not control.[2] They quickly realised forums were being monitored by PMs and players' narrative speculations were sometimes integrated into the game. This gave the impression the narrative was not set in stone, and players enjoyed knowing they could push PMs to make decisions they would not otherwise have made:

> *This is an interactive game, not a book or a movie. That mean[s] that we are in the driver's seat, to a degree.*
>
> (CM)

> *[. . .] it seems they may be listening to some of our speculations and incorporating them into the universe in subtle but interesting ways.*
>
> (CM)

> *It [the game] *is* fluid and flexible – swaying to move with what the players do . . . the PMs could never have known what people would have written and therefore had to wait until it was created by – us!!*
>
> (CM)

Accordingly, the power dynamic was relatively reciprocal, and players felt they could outsmart or challenge PMs, scrutinising updates for mistakes, intentional or otherwise. That they could sometimes gain an upper hand made them feel they had a stake in the story.

PMs confirmed that player affection for a character called the Red King prompted them to upgrade him to a more central role (Puppetmaster FAQ 2001). Some players questioned how much freedom they had to determine his fate:

> *PMs could have planned to have RK be saved. . . . However, if we don't get it right, if they want him to live, they definitely would have a backup storyline.*

(CM)

However, most were just excited to participate:

> *[. . .] today it's been kicked up a level by their placing a real person on the other end of the phone, not just a recording. How cool!*

(CM)

Some elements of agency were almost accidental – a whole storyline about an A.I. doppelganger was created because Cloudmakers spotted a stock photo that had been used twice (Puppetmaster FAQ 2001). However, they were rarely encouraged to create their own content, nor were they invited to determine the next stage in the narrative. The only exception was the Mann Act II, where players were asked to vote on legislation granting A.I.s the same rights as humans. ARGs are not choose-your-own-adventure style games, and the opportunities to 'pick a path' are limited.

No other ARGs so clearly incorporated player speculation into their narratives, but the chatter itself reflects Jenkins' notion of a fragmented story pulled together by player connections (2006: 121). This is also evident in links players made between plot points in WhySoSerious and *The Dark Knight*. Some were backed by textual analysis, for example, one spotted the Joker escaping the bank heist in a yellow school bus marked 'District 22', an area in which gothamusd.net had mentioned buses were being diverted.[3] Other connections seemed tenuous:

> *Members of a SWAT team use the phrases "shooting gallery" and "sitting ducks", while attempting to end a hostage crisis that the Joker concocts.*
>
> *Pasqualesbistro.com – The meeting between gang factions that takes place early in the film may occur in a back room of Pasquale's Bistro.*[4]

It is unclear whether these were intentional, but they allowed players to construct their own narratives and understandings of the alternate reality (and by extension the film itself) in a manner that reflected their lived experience of the game. Each speculation built another potential story layer, which ultimately defined how players understood the 'official' narrative in ways which could not be predetermined or controlled by PMs. With little narrative information available and conspiracy theory themes, Cloverfield and Super 8 players were even more inclined to fill the void with their own speculations.

The importance of narrative agency is most keenly felt when it is restricted. Neither WhySoSerious nor Super 8 allowed players to determine narrative outcomes, although action was required to push the story forwards. Super 8's levels of interactivity in this context were particularly limited. Christiano (2013) confirms player forums were monitored, but there were no adjustments to the storyline in response to player discussions. The lack of this kind of agency caused complaints from some players:

> *I also feel the 'finding' of things is left to the ARG characters rather than us and we just follow their reports.*
>
> (UF)

Even in what was ostensibly a highly interactive ARG, some WhySoSerious players felt the game had '*integrated the fans, but in a superficial way*' (SHH). Hon also highlighted that players don't have as much narrative control as they might think:

> You always know what you want players to do. . . . Sometimes they might do better than you think and that's wonderful and you might decide to go and change things . . . in Perplex City they liked one of our characters so much that we thought we'd keep her around a bit longer. . . . But they won't know whether they did that or not. Sometimes you might let them know by saying you need to email this person or they're going to die . . . if you make that threat they can respond in two ways and you plan for both of them. So they don't really have that much control in a way.
>
> (Hon 2012)

This seems at odds with Lee's claim that an ARG 'narrative is shaped – and ultimately owned – by the audience in ways that other forms of storytelling cannot match' (Lee cited in Rose 2007), or McGonigal's assertion that designers 'through ambiguity, must cede control over the final scope and dimensions of the game's solution to the players' (2008: 215). Indeed, her earlier work offers an almost contradictory model of this relationship:

> The gameplay of a puppet-mastered experience boils down to a high-stakes challenge: Perform or else. Or else what? Or else be denied the opportunity to play. . . . There is simply no optionality to the power play – do exactly what you're told or there is not play for you. This underlying power structure requires a level of overt submission from gamers that is simply unprecedented in game culture. And so the players' definition acknowledges: It is the puppetmasters, not the players, who 'control the game'.
>
> (McGonigal 2007)

She goes on to suggest this powerlessness is both pleasurable and wilful for players, comparing the pleasures of writing real-world missions to writing dramatic texts: 'Designing them in real time is very much the process of directing live actors on stage' (2007). The very term 'puppetmasters' suggests a power dynamic in favour of producers. But McGonigal's arguments reflect a tension between a desire to portray the games as democratic, and the reality that without significant PM control they become unplayable. A balance is required. To extend her original metaphor, actors may use their interpretations in their performances, but ultimately the director decides whether this interpretation is valid.

Stewart argues for a different approach, which avoids the risk of 'failstate' whereby the audience makes a decision (or fails to act at all), stalling or derailing the story entirely. Instead, he suggests ARGs offer 'the chance to affect or be seen or be reflected in the narrative' rather than actively controlling it. Players can 'see themselves in the story and register their impact in the story' (Stewart 2012). For example, in The Beast, players built a database of their own nightmares in reaction to a character called Loki, an A.I. who consumed dreams. Within 36 hours of the database appearing, Stewart wrote a soliloquy for Loki based on that database and developers created a Flash movie and voiceover. Stewart (2007) recalls 'watching people say "oh my god" and then "wait a minute, that's me." ' Instead of offering control, the story is 'responsive . . . acknowledges the audience's involvement. All those things *feel* really good and give the *sense* of ownership [my italics], but don't take you down the cul-de-sac of controlling events' (Stewart 2012). This allows for a level of productivity without making unrealistic claims for textual control.

Dena (2008) has a similar interpretation, viewing ARGs as:

> An emerging participatory practice that is not distinguished by any rewriting, modifying or amending the content of a primary producer.

Instead audiences co-create, filling in gaps left intentionally and unintentionally by the producer. Unlike well-documented . . . fan practices of extending the original narrative of a primary producer, the gaps to be filled are integral to the primary narrative.

Unlike Jenkins' 'textual poachers' (1992), this emphasises co-creation over appropriation, but the notion of gap-filling (particularly those gaps left intentionally) limits the amount of ownership players can claim over the content. They might fill these gaps in unexpected ways, or find unintended gaps to fill, but this remains a form of co-creation where producers largely retain authorial control of a text. There is little sense here of a fan community seeking to reclaim a text from the hands of its producers, yet like Stewart's scenario, it allows for meaningful if not radical productivity.

There are, arguably, other spaces where textual production occurs within ARGs that indicate players' influence on game content. McGonigal notes the plethora of player-created artefacts and networks without which the games are impossible to play, including 'wikis, group moderated blogs and multi-authored mailing lists, collaborative spreadsheets to list-servs, and toll-free online teleconferencing systems' (2008: 207). This is the production of systems and infrastructures to distribute and discuss 'official' content, without which that content is relatively pointless. It is also these systems which persist, whereas 'official' content is often removed from the web within a timeline specified by media companies. Other out-of-game, player-generated content includes parodies or spoofs of game materials, and merchandise such as t-shirts. Players even appropriate in-game content for their own use. McGonigal (2008) describes how players took ownership of Flea++ (an invented programming language in ilovebees) and used it in conversations outside the game. However, all these opportunities for textual production and meaning construction remain outside the 'official' text. What players create helps them navigate the game or speculate on meanings, but not necessarily change or add to that text in a way that circulates outside the community. This doesn't mean it's not important or useful to players in other ways, but it does not give them the kind of narrative control often being promised.

The illusion of inclusion

This all starts to suggest promotional ARGs offer an illusion of ownership and participation without allowing for any meaningful textual control, which is beneficial for media companies. ARGs may form part of an 'inhabitable' narrative world (Grainge 2008: 55–59), but since the industrial principle of Grainge's 'total entertainment' is one of near total ownership for conglomerates, audiences cannot play in that universe beyond the boundaries dictated by IP owners. The creative endeavour of 'worldbuilding' is therefore bound up with the more commercially oriented process of 'brand extension'. Christiano (2013) notes that the ARG for *Star Trek* was specifically charged with bringing in new audiences – 'to make Star Trek feel current, relevant, action, thriller. To shed all of those stereotypes'. It is less an opportunity for audiences to shape the meanings of those worlds than for producers emphasise a 'preferred reading' (Gray 2010: 72) of them via the promotional content. This is a highly negotiated kind of brand participation.

Stewart (2012) states, 'I think we have, without exaggeration, invented more ways for the audience to feel the illusion of control, than anyone in the world.' He finds the term 'illusion' overly pejorative, but it is strikingly difficult to find an alternative. The key issue is the suggestion that PMs and their corporate clients have somehow fooled players into thinking their participation matters on a narrative level, when in fact it has little impact.

Lee frequently discusses the importance of discovery for players. 'You. Who discovers that bizarre frame that's out of place on the TV, suddenly you own that experience. It's yours. You feel this tremendous sense of pride because you found it' (Lee cited in Ruberg 2006). This is the basis of viral marketing, which emphasises a sense of ownership of an experience (discovery) without owning any of the content involved in that experience. Passing on someone else's content makes you feel like part of it belongs to you because you 'activated' it.[5] That kind of exclusivity is hard to come by in a crowded Web 2.0 environment, so the stakes involved in being part of something like this are now significantly higher. Jenkins' (1992) textual poachers are powerful because their fan activity involves textual productivity that allows them to reclaim ownership of their fan texts. In *Convergence Culture* (2006), the collective intelligence of the hive mind allows them to make demands of producers regarding the kind of media products they want. In promotional ARGs, arguably the hive mind thinks it's a co-creator, when really it's just circulating other people's content for the benefit of someone else. This leaves players in a position of *dis*empowerment, moving closer towards one end of a dichotomy Hills (2002) identifies in fan studies. Fan activity is perceived as either resisting the consumer capitalist regimes of media corporations, or as free labour unwittingly enacted by fans whose collecting and purchasing habits play into the system rather than working against it.

However, for ARG players, this is emphatically an opt-in situation. One respondent even argued for the *importance* of *'the illusion of control, not necessarily the control itself'* (Survey Respondent #6). Sixty-seven percent of survey respondents expressed a desire for more narrative agency, yet the same percentage agreed PMs were ultimately in control of any ARG.

> *I worship player interaction and control over the direction of a story, even though I admit that, in reality, the Puppet Masters manipulate the players.*
>
> (UF)

Players knowingly concede a level of narrative control in return for a well-constructed, engaging entertainment experience. PMs, for their part, agree to provide those illusions via a responsive game design that respects that choice by doing 'everything in its power to make them not feel stupid about taking that leap with us' (Lee cited in Siegel 2006). Moreover, ARGs require the ability to simultaneously immerse oneself in the game world whilst analysing and critiquing it from the outside. To prod at the walls of an ARG is to acknowledge its construction. Players are unlikely to feel 'fooled' because they appreciate both the pleasures of the illusion and the context in which that illusion is created.

We might also question whether players even want this kind of power. Players of ilovebees were genuinely surprised to learn their actions affected the plot (Kim et al. 2008: 40). If players are not aware of their input, is it fair to describe this as part of the games' appeal? Hon (2012) also notes the creative dangers of offering players too many narrative paths to choose from. If burdened with endless decision-making, players become overwhelmed, and producers are tasked with providing content for every possible outcome. He argues players are more interested in being entertained than making decisions (2012). Forum discussion supports this, as players acknowledge the need to restrict agency to facilitate storytelling:

> *I see ARGs as the storytelling version of MMORPGs, where fundamental interaction is mostly sacrificed in order for a more detailed story to be told. . . .*
>
> (UF)

Player attitudes towards promotional games were certainly more flexible in this respect:

> *These ARGs are much less likely to bend to the will of players or give players any sense that the choices they make have any sort of impact since the final product (be it a TV show or movie or whatever) already exists . . . so it's more of an 'interactive fiction' story, where you plod along with the plot the PM has in mind and interact with it when*

necessary but nothing you do is actually going to show an impact to the end product.

(Survey Respondent #10)

Indeed, when asked for examples of players influencing the narrative, some mentioned promotional games run by 42 Entertainment, but none suggested Bad Robot/Paramount/Abrams ARGs, despite the Lost Experience and Cloverfield being prominent on the boards by this time (Nov./Oct. 2009). Most cited grassroots games, including Lockjaw and Eldritch Errors. There are fewer expectations for narrative agency in promotional ARGs, and some players were happy to look to grassroots games if this was important to them. However, as a result, promotional games started being referred to as 'just marketing' or 'just virals' rather than 'real' ARGs. As one player reflected on Super 8: '*This has been a hand fed Movie Viral from day one*' (UF).

Yet, another player echoes Hon's (2001) suggestion that even where narrative agency was lacking, players felt they made a difference:

Even going all the way back to The Beast, I think we can say by today's standards there was little to no interaction. Sure there was the Mike Royal call, but that's really the only example of direct one-on-one communication. Everything else was rather impersonal and to the community – the emails and phone calls were sent to any & all on the list. Even so, I'd be surprised if any of the players felt that they didn't have an impact on the story or the universe.

(UF)

Örnebring (cited in IGDA 2006) suggests:

ARGs could be viewed as part of an ongoing contestation of narrative, where (fan) audiences increasingly feel that they have (or ought to have) some measure of ownership over a text, and where media organisations, faced with a world of easy-access downloading and file sharing, increasingly want to retain control over their intellectual property.

If narrative control is key to 'ownership of a media text', this is an impossible goal for ARG players, and one they do not anticipate a promotional ARG can achieve. Seventy-five percent of survey respondents reported a strong sense of ownership over ARGs they played. However, they were split regarding the relationship between ownership and narrative control. Half agreed the two were linked but the other half either disagreed or remained neutral on the question.

Stewart's proposition of being 'seen' in the text is an augmentation of the relationship, which does not take control as its central problem. A text instead responds to and respects an audience, which it acknowledges to be active, knowledgeable, and in possession of the means to participate but ultimately wants to be taken on a journey more than it wants the power to map that journey out. If players are doing all the work, who is entertaining who? It seems the feeling of agency is indeed more important than actual authorial control. ARGs provide a middle ground in this 'ongoing contestation', satisfying players' need for that illusion whilst allowing IP owners to retain a comfortable level of control.

It is therefore not solely located in narrative agency but other aspects of ARGs that provide space for players to feel ownership and empowerment in their role as audience. One surveyed player suggested this sense of ownership came from *'the give and take, call-and-response mechanics along with the feeling of community'* (Survey Respondent #2). Here, ownership is related to an affective connection which can be prompted by other elements of an ARG.

Affective connections – characters, communities, and PMs

Storytelling is an intrinsically affective process and strong conveyor of emotions. Advertising is similarly described in terms of 'telling a story' rather than 'selling a product' in its attempts to communicate brand values that connect with consumers' feelings, aspirations, and ideals. Advocates suggested this approach appealed to media-saturated consumers because 'there's subtlety in having the brand live underneath a story' (Horlick cited in Boswell 2002). As storytelling, ARGs are therefore somewhat affective already, amplifying this by telling their stories through personal media channels: 'When I get a text message on my cell phone from this game it feels personal to me in a way mass communication doesn't' (McGonigal cited in Irwin 2007). This brings the marketing message out of the public domain and starts to encroach on the private space of players who must actively invite the game into that sphere. Whilst that might seem intrusive, this came at a time when many consumers were developing their own online presences and social media was increasingly blurring the lines between public and private.

This affective connection allows for a mode of personal empowerment reflected in Grossberg's (1992) model of fandom based on an 'affective sensibility'. He suggests a fan's relation to the chosen text 'operates in the domain of affect or mood' (1992: 56). For Grossberg, affect is not the equivalent of emotion or desire, but the 'feeling of life . . . Affect is what gives "colour", "tone" or "texture" to our experiences' (1992: 57). This feeling places objects, practices, and meanings on our 'mattering maps' (1992: 57). The elevated status of the text on the fan's 'mattering map' allows its use as a locus for the fan's own identity. Grossberg views this as a form of empowerment via popular culture, describing fandom as a potential site of 'optimism, invigoration and passion' (1992: 65). This can translate into popular struggle and political resistance, which are otherwise 'likely to be drowned in the sea of historical pessimism' (Grossberg 1992: 65). We can see this optimism in elements of promotional ARGs beyond narrative control or authorship, allowing not only for a sense of textual ownership, but a more personal form of empowerment. Even if that passion and optimism does not translate into political change, its potential and energy is still important.

The games were gripping enough to work their way into the personal lives of many players, evidenced in forum posts about losing sleep waiting for updates, playing at work, putting off schoolwork, or ensuring the game did not encroach on family commitments:

> *Today I cancelled a fairly important meeting because it was more important to hang* [out] *here and wait for 10.*
> *I did the same thing!*
>
> (SHH)

Addiction metaphors were common. In a dedicated thread on SHH titled 'Official TDK Viral Marketing Support Group', players light-heartedly swapped stories of their difficulties at the end of the game:

> *I checked the wiki this morning. . . . I checked the wiki two minutes ago . . . when I wake up I know I'll check it. . . . I don't control my compulsion, my compulsion controls me Just one last taste, one last taste of viral goodness.*
>
> (SHH)

Many favourite game moments were those shared with friends or family, again emphasising the position of the games on Grossberg's (1992) 'mattering maps':

> *[. . .] the recent Dark Knight screening because I got to share it with Giskard who was visiting from the Netherlands.*
>
> (UF)

> *The small favours task in Last Call Poker. I brought my daughter along and it turned out to be one of the most memorable moments of her life (she was three at the time).*
>
> (UF)

Affective connections were also made between players and characters. This is not new or unusual, but the opportunity to interact with characters made this connection more intense:

> *I know players who were deeply saddened and disturbed by the death of some (well-written) characters in the games, and in one case players went out of their way to make SURE that one character DID NOT DIE.*
>
> (UF)

> *. . . one of the best parts of ARGs is the communication between players and characters. People get a sort of rush by talking to someone they know has secrets. What are they going to reveal? How can I gain their trust? Could I get another website out of them? It's this small, euphoric high that drives some people to play these games.*
>
> (UF)

Survey respondents also selected community as the third most important element of an ARG, behind puzzle solving and storytelling. When asked to describe their relationships with other players, responses were overwhelmingly positive. The intensity varied from casual friendships to Stewart's (2012) recollections of attending the wedding of two players who met during The Beast. The community is central to the enjoyment of an ARG:

> *I love the community that forms around a well-developed and presented game . . . gives me a sense of being part of 'something bigger'.*
>
> (UF)

> *ARGs are, to me, all about becoming a part of something bigger and getting to engage directly with the community of players.*
>
> (Survey Respondent #11)

> *The community, the co-operative aspect of ARGs is a big part of what keeps me at least coming back here.*
>
> (UF)

There is a real sense of collective empowerment and inclusiveness through collaborative play. Even seemingly insignificant input felt valuable:

> *I'm not personally the best puzzle solver . . . but working together I get to feel like a hero by getting specific aspects sometimes.*
>
> (Survey Respondent #6)

McGonigal (2008) similarly suggests ARGs allow everyone to feel they have contributed to the group's success: 'The plausibility of so many diverse interpretations empowered players of all skill levels, natural abilities, inclinations and interest to achieve success . . . no player is left out . . . no individual discouraged or excluded from the opportunity to contribute to participatory culture' (2008: 215).

This argument is often put forward by what Hesmondhalgh (2013: 313) calls 'digital optimists', but he feels the limitations of this inclusive vision are not fully interrogated. It fails to consider the high barrier to entry, difficulty in joining a real-time game in its latter stages, internal community hierarchies/competition, and the reality that not everyone gets to contribute. This is therefore not a universally beneficial form of empowerment.

However, it is possible that even loosely being part of a community is enough for consumers to experience a feeling of participation and inclusion, which may even benefit consumer brands:

> An ARG basically says . . . we make you part of a group and we do it in such a way that the success of anyone in the group is felt as the success of the entire group. When a CM solves a puzzle all the CMs say 'we're awesome!' Old Spice Guy is a tremendously successful example of something lighter that nonetheless makes people feel involved. When one person has their question answered by Old Spice Guy, everyone watching the Old Spice Guy says 'hey, look, we're on TV!' We select one person to stand in for the people and if the people really feel that person is their surrogate then they feel responded to. I think for brands of all kinds there's value for them in having that sort of connection.
>
> (Stewart 2012)

It would be difficult to describe Old Spice consumers as a brand community since, as Stewart (2012) points out, the concept relies on that brand becoming a 'tool of self-expression' or 'the empowerment of a person's ability to project themselves into the world.' Indeed, 70% of surveyed players disagreed with the description of ARG communities as 'brand communities'. Yet they employ tactics that might encourage the formation of such a community. A study of promotional forums and websites launched by Nutella suggests this is possible with household brands (Cova & Pace 2006). Furthermore, ARGs encourage players to create these spaces themselves (Yahoo! Boards for The Beast, Unfiction for Super 8) or use spaces and networks they have already built (SHH for WhySoSerious), allowing them to feel more control over that community. Rules forbidding PMs to participate in that community strengthen that feeling of ownership.

In a Web 2.0 context, ARGs often tap into existing networks such as Facebook or Twitter over which players have less control. Stewart (2012) describes these as 'porch' space – semi-private/public spaces where people feel comfortable performing personalities and identities (including brand affiliations) through liking, retweeting, or mentioning them. The increase in their use in ARGs is symptomatic of an approach which presumes anything received through those channels automatically feels more personalised or has greater affective impact. The reality is that although this might be possible, they are now as saturated with advertising as TV channels and a more creative approach is needed if they are to be used effectively. They might offer a link to vast audiences, but they are neither a shortcut to a network of undiscerning eyes, nor a guarantee of affective connections or brand loyalty, which must be more carefully cultivated. Brands continue to seek acceptance in them, often via brand ambassadors or influencers, especially in spaces like YouTube and Instagram (Burns 2016), but the level of intrusion means an authentic brand community is less likely to develop. This cannot be manufactured because ultimately consumers must construct and maintain that group themselves for it to be authentic. The ability to form a meaningful brand community is therefore in the hands of consumers, although an ARG can provide the starting point for that affective relationship to develop.

They may not have been cultivating a brand community, but PMs on The Beast did observe player forums closely and became familiar with key players and moderators (Puppetmaster FAQ 2001). They regarded players with affection as collaborators in a new genre of storytelling and met with them on several occasions post-game, flying moderators out to Seattle as a gesture of thanks. Fifty-five percent of surveyed players agreed ARGs could be described as an 'intensely felt, emotionally affecting experience'.[6] Players therefore had to trust PMs would not design games that took advantage of or made light of those affective investments. The relationship needed to be based on mutual trust and respect and was described by survey respondents as *'collaborative'* (#12) and *'symbiotic'* (#35).

This trust enabled further affective investments to be made, which in turn enabled the sense of ownership or empowerment around the games. The relationship was initially highly responsive, with the onus on PMs to modify the game according to player behaviour. It was a genuinely give-take situation which intimated to players that their actions mattered. Moreover, it inferred a level at which power was shared between the two sides:

> *Tango – one may be leading the other at any given time but ultimately the dance is done together.*

> (Survey Respondent #6)

Like jazz musicians, playing off each other. NOT like two chess players playing against each other.

(Survey Respondent #2)

Performer and audience . . . but in both directions.

(Survey Respondent #22)

Both are the dancer, both are the musician, and both play the roles of performer/audience simultaneously. Both are active in creation, neither retains a passive role. This feedback loop is not necessarily new. Stewart likens the experience to 'Dickens writing serial novels for the newspapers with a public exclaiming over each instalment as you wrote the next' (Cloudmakers 2001). However, the visibility of audiences online intensifies that loop as players express themselves clearly and swiftly on forums at any stage in their consumption processes. Lee (cited in Ruberg 2006) therefore views ARGs as part of a broader move in the industry to respond to the closing gap between producers and audiences.

Early games often involved post-game chats between PMs and players, in which PMs were keen to relate to players as equals. Live chats were conducted via instant messenger, so there was scope to pre-prepare or edit answers, but transcripts suggest this was a relatively direct and honest exchange. It took place in internet relay channels used by players during the game, so PMs were effectively meeting fans on their own turf. PMs also adopted player-created language, highlighting a shared culture:

> Elan – Well, we touched on this a bit earlier on (sorry for the trout).

(Cloudmakers 2001)[7]

This dialogue continued in events such as ARGFest, where the tone was relaxed and informal. Players behaved fannishly towards PMs and PMs responded with deference:

> Player – how do you guys feel about suddenly going from authors, web designers etc, to duly worshipped heroes in the eyes of 7500 people worldwide?
>
> Elan – it's been pretty overwhelming, seeing as how my only previous exposure to fame as been my friends thinking that my car is pretty cool
>
> Sean – And of course there was the 140000 eyed copy editor and bs-detector roving hungrily like a band of jackals across a battle field, keeping all the continuity in line Thank you, thank you, thank you

Elan – We wanted this to be big and you guys made it huge! We wanted it to be pretty and you guys made it gorgeous. We wanted it to be enduring and you guys made it permanent. This really wouldn't be anything without you guys.

(Cloudmakers 2001)

This may look like a unique mode of engagement, but it reflects existing theories of relationship marketing (RM), perhaps taken to new levels. RM develops long-term customer loyalty and is focussed on the importance of trust. However, the intensity of this relationship in an ARG is not sustainable from a labour or cost perspective. As a result, it was not as personal during WhySoSerious or Super 8. Admittedly, WhySoSerious was much larger in scale, involving international events and promoting a globally recognised franchise. If ARGs are designed to reach a broad audience, it seems unfair to expect them to simultaneously be highly personalised experiences. By the time Super 8 arrived, players had lowered their expectations for promotional ARGs accordingly:

I think that for larger marketing ARGs the relationship is less intimate now, but grassroots games still exist that maintain that sort of relationship.

(Survey Respondent #28)

Movie marketing has moved away from the early ARG model precisely because the relationship needed to change as the size of the audience grew.

(Survey Respondent #8)

There was no visible interaction between players and PMs and no post-game discussion. Players by and large accepted this as inevitable, but trust is difficult to maintain without that feedback loop. Hills argues fan 'trust' is central to the creation and maintenance of the 'cult' in relation to the 'ontological security of the text (2002: 138). Fans continually test the hyperdiegetic world for breaks in continuity, logic, or consistency in the textual universe. They can then develop a secure relationship with the text in which they may embark on identity management and affective play (Hills 2002: 128). This is where more restrictive ARGs come up short. Trust in solid textual construction requires trust in the architects of that world, whether that is perceived to be 42 Entertainment or J.J. Abrams. Without this, the game collapses in a practical, structural sense and loses credibility for players as a space in which meaningful affective play can take place. Without that affective play, it is harder to claim consumer empowerment as Grossberg (1992) conceptualises it.

In the initial stages of the genre's evolution, several elements of this relationship disrupted Hills' (2002) incorporated/resistant dichotomy. The realtime interactions, rules set by both parties, and the opportunity (albeit limited) for players to impact the game's narrative suggest the potential for consumers to make more demands of producers in the way that Jenkins (2006) envisages. The Beast had proven media producers could sustain affective and responsive relationships with consumers, yet this element of ARGs has increasingly been suppressed. If this feedback loop initially told player communities what they did mattered, restricting it told them that, really, it didn't. As this relationship weakens, so does the potential for consumer empowerment via promotional ARGs. This is perhaps inevitable, but the more responsive that relationship is, the more power we can claim for audiences via Jenkins' model of participatory culture. Reinstating that distance might be motivated by practicalities, but it changes the power dynamic in ways which mean players cannot have that kind of empowered relationship with producers.

Affective investments and real-world impact

Affective play within an ARG may affect decision-making behaviours in players' real lives, the two of which exist in close proximity in a genre which blurs the line between fiction and reality. The clearest link to Grossberg's (1992) arguments about the practical potential of affective empowerment was the heartfelt belief amongst many players that the hive mind could solve real-world problems. The most striking example of this is the case of some Cloudmakers who, in the hours following the attacks on the World Trade Center in September 2001, discussed the possibility of using their collective knowledge to 'solve the puzzle of who the terrorists are' (McGonigal 2003: 1). Other Cloudmakers quickly became unsettled with the apparent slippage between play and a terrifying real-life situation. Group moderators eventually released an announcement requesting discussions of 'solving' 9/11 be concluded. McGonigal argues that, for many, working with the Cloudmakers had 'profoundly affected their sense of identity and purpose, to the point that a game mentality was a natural response to real-world events' (2003: 1). She further suggests that although players might be overoptimistic in their ability to solve such problems, the lingering effects of collective gaming can change players' perspectives on real-world situations (2003: 7). She argues for it to be considered for its 'radical political potential and creative, generative possibilities of multiple social formation and interaction' (2003: 9). One player also discussed the possibility of contributing to the investigation of Norwegian murderer Anders Breivik:

Not an ARG, but needs some work nevertheless. . . . The guys over at Reddit are working on cracking what the Norweigan police apparently think might be a code in Breiviks manifesto – gps-coordinates, disguised as html-links and scattered with cryptic text. . . . I realise that Unforums deal with fictional events and that Breivik is as real as it gets, but you guys are crazy good at coorperating and picking each other's brains to figure stuff like this out. Perhaps you should have a go at it.

(UF)

Such conjectures were often curbed by the community itself and rarely resulted in action. But even players who strongly felt this was not within the remit of the player community believed it could be attempted:

If CM were so inclined to solve world hunger, I'm sure we could take a stab at it, although it's subjective on the successfulness of such a quest. If we wanted to send our crack theories of terrorism based on Google results, I'm sure we'd find someone to send them too. This group as a whole does not want to do these things. Get over it.

(CM)

The most important impact of such discussions is more subjective; a form of empowerment akin to Grossberg's sense of 'the generation of energy and passion . . . the construction of possibility' (1992: 64). Players felt they collectively or individually had an ability to make a difference through their participation in the game, whether that possibility translated into action or not. This is not the intended result of promotional ARGs and realistically has no value to marketers, but is significant to players who can and do receive these games as something other than marketing.

Self-identity, personal and professional development

As Stewart notes, brands which can support a community tend to be those which consumers feel express something about their identities or lifestyles. This makes it difficult to apply the term to any and all consumer products:

Something at the heart of a community is social and aspirational . . . a Jag invites me into an aspirational world. . . . But soap? Hard to see. . . . You might like the brand but that's a tough lapel pin.

(Stewart 2012)

However, ARGs can allow space for consumers to use branded content in a process of self-definition. This is not the case for all players, but it exists nonetheless. This lends an element of the subcultural to ARG communities. Most understandings of subculture revolve around the appropriation of cultural symbols to create counter-hegemonic meanings and identities, despite acknowledging that not all subcultures are necessarily oppositional (Hebdige 1988; Thornton 2005; During 2007). For promotional ARGs, the process is more about the appropriation of a commercial text to furnish a sense of self-identity not just as a fan, but as puzzle solver, detective, communicator, team-player, community member, or even superhero:

> Your superpower is simply that you notice this cool thing that most people don't notice. . . . There's something very empowering about saying there's a little bit of magic in this world and if you pay attention you'll find it. . . . Oh my god, a phone's ringing! Maybe it's someone who needs to talk to me because only I can save the day. So we try to say yeah, only you can save the day, and that phone ringing is for you so answer it.
>
> (Lee cited in Siegel 2006)

Such appropriation may not be radical, oppositional, or even widespread, but some players do find meanings in ARGs they can relate to their own personal experiences and identities. One player claims: '*At a fundamental level, my identity as a player reflects who I am and what I believe*' (CM). This kind of relationship with a media text lies fundamentally in the hands of consumers rather than producers and cannot be brought into being by sheer force. It is players who decide whether the game and/or associated brand speaks to them in this personal manner.

ARGs can also help players develop new or existing skills. These could be technical or knowledge-based skills learned in the process of playing. For example, one player enjoyed learning '*about aspects of cryptography through creative puzzles*' (Survey Respondent #31). Others developed interpersonal skills that were transferable to their working lives:

> *I have learned that everyone has different strengths and weaknesses and that sometimes, I have to leave it up to other to do, because they are better at it than I am (this is a HUGE thing for me, as I am forced to supervise my employees from a distance for the past 6 months, and thanks to people here, I have become a better supervisor, my heartfelt thanks!).*
>
> (UF)

It significantly changed the way one player managed personal and professional relationships:

> *I've learned a great deal about being part of a functioning community. I know that my attitude towards other people has changed – my*

*expectations are that people will help each other, people care about
each other. I didn't feel that way before.*

(UF)

Others used these skills to develop their own grassroots games, and several lead moderators in player communities now work in professional transmedia roles and founded their own companies. Lead CM Moderators Adrian Hon, Dan Hon, and Andrea Phillips are all prominent transmedia professionals, and Steve Peters (Chief Moderator on ilovebees) founded No Mimes Media. Evidently this is not the experience of every player, but it is indicative of the impact of promotional ARGs outside their marketing context. However, this experience could be read more cynically as unpaid labour, providing media companies with a new generation of workers without footing the bill for training and development. Moreover, these creatives go on to work for corporate clients. So, whilst these skills do not initially provide value for corporates, players-turned-puppetmasters can still find themselves on the payroll for companies who profit from their earlier unpaid labour.

All these responses reflect the significance of the ability (real or perceived) to take some control or ownership over a story universe, or at least to be considered a part of it that matters. ARGs encourage elaborated forms of self-consciousness and self-reflection, dispelling stereotypes of gamers as overly introverted or inward-looking (Jenkins 1992). As players become rigorously analytical of their own in-/out-of-game behaviours, ARGs become increasingly personal spaces where they can reflect upon their own identities. The 'reality' element of an ARG, combined with the fact that you play as yourself and not as an avatar, enhances this feeling. In the context of a marketing campaign, this could help fans and wider audiences feel more important and recognised as individuals within a mainstream media landscape that has historically treated them as faceless groups to be sold to – whether as one homogenous 'mass' audience or a number of market 'segments'. However, these feelings of empowerment reside firmly outside of that context, in a more personal and subjective realm.

Conclusion

The relationship between players and PMs implies ongoing negotiations of power and mutual dependence, but further analysis reveals a complex dynamic which may change depending on IP, expectations of the community, and affordances of game design. Power may shift between the two parties but can never be said to lie exclusively on one side. It is important to acknowledge the limitations of promotional ARGs in this respect, but not at the expense of recognising the audience's ability to choose not to play, or their limited ability to impact the text.

The insistence on correlating power with content control, whilst understandable and an important issue, means the possibilities for other forms of empowerment are not given serious enough consideration. Promotional ARGs reveal that, as Grossberg argues, an 'active' audience does not always mean an audience in 'control' of a text (1992: 54), or even a productive audience. Being active and participating in a media text in a contemporary media landscape spans a wide spectrum of activities including lurking, tweeting, liking, remixing, writing fan fiction, and producing fan videos or websites. Consumer empowerment is too often characterised as textual or political, and the potential for this kind of empowerment via participatory marketing practices like ARGs is slim. Producers ultimately retain control of the text, and that is overwhelmingly acknowledged and, to a certain extent, accepted by consumers. Collectively they might have a louder voice, but since the limitations of their participation are set by producers, so are the boundaries and terms of their apparent emancipation.

But ARG players can claim alternative forms of personal and social empowerment, outside the realms of textual productivity. They can develop new modes of thinking about the world that genuinely change the way they relate to it and to other people living in it. They can claim new understandings of themselves and their skills and capabilities. This is no less important or influential than their ability to demand changes to media texts, or the ways they are made and marketed. This is a result of their participation and a form of empowerment that gets left behind in discussions because it is not a radical renegotiation of the power relationship between producers and consumers. Instead ARGs reveal a continual, subtle negotiation of power, which constitutes a unique version of the player/producer relationship.

The decline in more responsive game design does, however, suggest this was an innovative and exciting experiment, rather than something sustainable in the long term, particularly within the framework of Hollywood's industrial logic. The potential for this renegotiation of power is also reduced dramatically when interactivity is reduced or when players feel exploited. 'Meaningful' participation does not have to equate to control of media texts; it is less meaningful when working purely in the service of a brand or ad company. In these contexts, it's possible to see players as being disempowered because their investments are fundamentally being co-opted and their energy and labour exploited to create value for media corporations. The next chapter looks more closely at this argument and asks how players and producers conceptualise the value of their participation and whether it might point to a more complex kind of digital labour than established arguments allow for.

Notes

1 In mathematics and the arts, two quantities are in the golden ratio (φ) if the ratio of the sum of the quantities to the larger quantity is equal to the ratio of the larger quantity to the smaller one.
2 Control was also a narrative theme of The Beast. The game frequently asked players to question how far humans could expect to control A.I.s and how much free will they should be allowed.
3 https://batman.wikibruce.com/Film_references
4 https://batman.wikibruce.com/Film_references
5 The term 'activation' is a recent marketing buzzword. Brands using involving immersive or participatory tactics tend to refer to 'brand activations' as opposed to launches. The phrase evokes the notion of bringing a brand 'to life' but often involves the consumer audience doing some 'activating' themselves, via social media or interacting with in-store or site-specific installations.
6 Taken from Matt Hills' definition of 'cult' fandoms (Hills 2002: x).
7 Cloudmakers invented a word to describe 'the polite response to a redundant or factually false post. The word "trout" is a term of respect.' It was intended to make newcomers feel more at home on forums when they asked questions, for example, about puzzles that had already been solved. https://groups.yahoo.com/neo/groups/cloudmakers/conversations/messages/6591

References

Boswell, K. (2002) 'Telling Good Stories: How the AI Online Campaign Kicked Viral Marketing Over the Fence to Us All', *The Marketleap Report*, 2(4). Available: www.marketleap.com/report/ml_report_23.htm [Accessed 24.06.2009]. No longer available online. Print copy held by author.
Burns, K. (2016) 'How the Top Social Media Brands Use Influencer and Brand Advocacy Campaigns to Engage Fans', in A. Hutchins & N. Tindall, eds., *Public Relations and Participatory Culture*, London: Routledge.
Christiano, J. (2013) *Email Interview with Author*, 6.03.2013.
Cloudmakers. (2001) *Post-Game Puppetmaster Chat*, 31.07.2001. Available: http://groups.yahoo.com/neo/groups/cloudmakers/files [Accessed 11.01.2019].
Cova, B. & Pace, S. (2006) 'Brand community of convenience products: new forms of customer empowerment - the case 'my Nutella the Community'', *European Journal of Marketing*, 40:9, pp. 1087–1105.
Dena, C. (2008) *Anti Hoaxing Strategies and the TINAG Fallacy*. Available: www.christydena.com/2008/01/anti-hoaxing-strategies-and-the-tinag-fallacy/ [Accessed 17.01.2019].
During, S. E. (2007) *The Cultural Studies Reader*, 3rd Edition, London: Routledge.
Gallagher, D. F. (2001) 'Some Prefer Online "A.I." Tie-In to the Movie', *The New York Times*, 09.07.2001. Available: www.nytimes.com/2001/07/09/technology/09GAME.html [Accessed 05.01.2019].
Gilmore, J. & Pine, J. (1998) 'Welcome to the Experience Economy', *Harvard Business Review*, 07.08.1998.

Gray, J. (2010) *Show Sold Separately: Promos, Spoilers, and Other Media Paratexts*, New York, NY.: New York University Press.

Grossberg, L. (1992) 'Is There a Fan in the House? The Affective Sensibility of Fandom', in L. A. Lewis, ed., *The Adoring Audience*, London: Routledge, pp. 50–68.

Hall, S. (1973) *Encoding and Decoding in the Television Discourse*, Birmingham: The University of Birmingham, Birmingham Centre for Contemporary Cultural Studies.

Hebdige, D. (1988) *Hiding in the Light: On Images and Things*, London: Comedia.

Hesmondhalgh, D. (2013) *The Cultural Industries*, 3rd Edition, London: Sage.

Hills, M. (2002) *Fan Cultures*, London; New York, NY: Routledge.

Hon, A. (2001) *The Guide*, 09.2001. Available: http://web.archive.org/web/20060 116100956/www.cloudmakers.org:80/guide/ [Accessed 11.01.2019].

Hon, A. (2012) *Interview with Author*, 26.10.2012, London.

IGDA ARG SIG. (2006) *Alternate Reality Games SIG/Whitepaper International Games Developers Association*. Available: www.christydena.com/wp-content/uploads/2007/11/igda-alternaterealitygames-whitepaper-2006.pdf [Accessed 21. 04.2019].

Irwin, M. J. (2007) 'Q&A with Alternate Reality Games Director Elan Lee', *Wired Magazine*, 15(6), 17.05.2007. Available: https://web.archive.org/web/20130614215450/www.wired.com/gaming/virtualworlds/magazine/15-06/st_arg3 [Accessed 11.01.2019].

Jenkins, H. (1992) *Textual Poachers: Television Fans & Participatory Culture*, New York, NY; London: Routledge.

Jenkins, H. (2006) *Convergence Culture: Where Old and New Media Collide*, New York, NY: New York University Press.

Kim, J. Y., Allen, J. P. & Lee, E. (2008) 'Alternate Reality Gaming', *Communications of the ACM*, 51(2), pp. 36–42. Available: http://cacm.acm.org/magazines/2008/2/5456-alternate-reality-gaming/fulltext [Accessed 05.01.2015].

McGonigal, J. (2003) 'This Is Not a Game: Immersive Aesthetics & Collective Play', Paper presented at Melbourne Digital Arts & Culture Conference. Available: https://janemcgonigal.files.wordpress.com/2010/12/mcgonigal-jane-this-is-not-a-game.pdf [Accessed 18.04.2019].

McGonigal, J. (2007) 'The Puppetmaster Problem: Design for Real World, Mission Based Gaming', in P. Harrigan & N. Wardrip-Fruin, eds., *Second Person*, Cambridge, MA.; London: MIT Press.

McGonigal, J. (2008) 'Why I Love Bees: A Case Study in Collective Intelligence Gaming', in K. Salen, ed., *The Ecology of Games*, Cambridge, MA; London: MIT Press, pp. 199–227.

McKee, A. (2013) 'The Power of Art, the Power of Entertainment', *Media, Culture and Society*, 35(6), pp. 759–770.

Puppetmaster FAQ. (2001) Available: http://web.archive.org/web/20020810185009/http://familiasalla-es.cloudmakers.org:80/credits/note/faq.html [Accessed 11.01. 2019].

Rose, F. (2007) 'Secret Website, Coded Messages: The New World of Immersive Games', *Wired Magazine*, 16(1). Available: www.wired.com/entertainment/music/magazine/16-01/ff_args [Accessed 11.01.2019].

Ruberg, B. (2006) 'Elan Lee's Alternate Reality', *Gamasutra.com*. Available: www.gamasutra.com/view/feature/130182/elan_lees_alternate_reality.php [Accessed 11.01.2019].

Siegel, S. J. (2006) 'Joystiq Interviews Elan Lee of 42 Entertainment', *Joystiq.com*, 14.11.2006. Available: www.engadget.com/2006/11/14/joystiq-interviews-elan-lee-of-42-entertainment [Accessed 11.01.2019].

Smith, N. (2008) 'Following the Scent', *New Media Age*, pp. 23–24, 09.10.2008.

Stewart, S. (2007) *ARGFest Transcript 06 – Roundtable – 42 Entertainment – Development Process Part II*. Available: https://web.archive.org/web/20070510222718/http://wiki.argfestocon.com:80/index.php?title=2007vt06_Transcription [Accessed 15.01.2019].

Stewart, S. (2012) *Interview with Author*, 10.12.2012, London.

Thornton, S. (2005) 'The Social Logic of Subcultural Capital', in Ken Gelder, ed., *The Subcultures Reader*, New York, NY: Routledge.

4   Promotional ARGs and digital labour

The relationship between players and producers of promotional ARGs involves a distinct give and take in terms of power relations, partially due to the real-time nature of the games. This allows players to develop affective, emotional connections to their ARG experiences, making their participation more powerful and resonant. Their sense of being able to affect the narrative of the game might be described as 'illusory', but those emotional investments are very real. There may not be a dramatic shift in the balance of media power, but that's not to say the games are not productive and valuable for players in other ways.

However, these investments of time and emotion are inextricably connected to what could be described as unpaid digital marketing labour. Arguably, promotional ARGs exploit consumers' energies and emotional labour in the service of conglomerates like Warner Bros. These debates are not new, and there are numerous studies regarding the co-optation of fan labour by media companies (Andrejevic 2008; de Kosnik 2013; Chin 2014; Bakioğlu 2018). This also relates to broader discussions about the digital economy and exploitation of the 'free labour' of internet workers and users (Terranova 2000; Scholz 2013).

Promotional ARGs complicate this discussion. This labour occurs in commercial, branded spaces, but also in fan-constructed forums including Unfiction or Superherohype.com, making it difficult to claim any straightforward co-optation of those spaces and the work that happens in them. Previous work in this area often results in binary arguments that view these activities as either exploiting fans' labour or providing genuine opportunities for their participation in media properties. Promotional ARGs suggest the reality for fans and audiences is not that simple. Most players are aware of their role in a marketing campaign; few are under the illusion that their activities are disconnected from a wider system of consumer capitalism. Survey data and analysis of player forum discussions point to an active negotiation of their position in this relationship. This breaks down that dichotomy and presents a messier but more accurate representation of their 'lived experiences' of ARGs (Hills 2002: 35).

This chapter questions whether we can describe the 'work' of promotional ARG players as 'free labour' or 'exploitation' as these terms have previously been conceptualised. Informed by Hills (2002) and Hesmondhalgh (2010), this discussion considers perspectives of players undertaking this work, and how they perceive the value of their labour. It examines the roles of 'swag', the gifting economy, relationship marketing, and the player/PM relationship. The latter significantly affects how players view not only their own labour, but the labour of game designers. It allows them to view PMs almost as allies, with the same aims, goals, and priorities for ARGs, which do not align with those of marketers. This also highlights an interesting dynamic whereby players identify strongly with PMs in their apparently shared labouring, which almost functions to justify their own work.

ARG labour

To identify what 'work' ARG players are doing, we can look to Terranova's influential definition of 'free labour', which includes:

> the activity of building Web sites, modifying software packages, reading and participating in mailing lists, and building virtual spaces on MUDs [multi-user dungeons]. . . . It is about specific forms of production (Web design, multimedia production, digital services, and so on), but it is also about forms of labor we may not immediately recognise as such: chat, real-life stories, mailing lists, amateur newsletters, and so on.
>
> (Terranova 2000)

Terranova's categories refer primarily to early internet user activities but are still relevant to most or all of the following activities undertaken by promotional ARG players:

Forum/website construction and maintenance – An infrastructure is required for the hive mind to gather in if collaborative games are to function. Cloudmakers formed a Yahoo! Group which was moderated and monitored by player administrators. Players sacrificed both time and money to run Unfiction.com. Hosting and development costs were funded by the site's founder and supplemented by donations and sales of Unfiction merchandise.[1] Several moderators also monitored forums and maintained community regulations. Steve Peters, moderator of the grassroots game Lockjaw, also developed Alternate Reality Gaming Network (ARGN). Players of Super 8 gathered at Super8news.com/forums, developed by the creators of

Cloverfield ARG community cloverfieldnews.com. None of these spaces existed before the games began, and none were run with any involvement from PMs or their corporate clients.

Puzzle solving/storytelling/speculation/chat – This is effectively the 'playing' of an ARG. The involvement of individual players varies, but as a community they invest time, energy, and creativity, particularly in speculation and chat. Their visibility allows marketers to better understand the expectations and values of the fan community and circulates further word of mouth about the film. This can amount to providing free market research for media companies.

Wiki creation/maintenance – Players created wiki pages to outline developments for newcomers to the long and complex ARG narratives.[2] A player guide for The Beast was also constructed by lead Cloudmaker moderator Adrian Hon. The Guide and accompanying list of in-game sites (The Trail), became key resources for players and puppetmasters alike: 'The up side of this enormous, beady-eyed, voracious player-monster was that less than a week after the *A.I.* trailer hit the Web, CM and The Trail were our definitive continuity source' (Puppetmaster FAQ 2001). These were detailed documents and required extensive commitment to keep them updated throughout long-running campaigns.

User Generated Content (UGC) – Official and Unofficial – Wikis and speculation could be considered 'unofficial' UGC – content players developed for their own enjoyment, or to keep track of the game. Other examples include Super 8's Rocket Poppeteers spreadsheet, which logged scores from the mini Flash games, and a wonderfully detailed website dedicated to whysoserious.[3] This performed an archival function, which many players were keen to promote given the ephemeral nature of the games. Others discussed making physical scrapbooks, and Super 8 players produced their own merchandise including mugs, t-shirts, and stickers, all of which were collaboratively designed with careful consideration of legal ramifications:

> We should play it on the safe side and try to stay away from verbiage or logos which might tend to imply anything directly about the IP (intellectual property) of JJ Abrams, Spielberg, and Paramount. We here as fans created the 'We Must Party' slogan relative to the film, so it's ours.
>
> (UF)

There was also 'official' UGC – content which was firmly in game and requested by PMs. For example, players were asked to submit pictures of their 'sightings of Batman' to Citizensforbatman.org. This kind of content production lies more obviously within the realms of marketing work. It is required to progress the game and players are almost always asked to share it via social media channels, providing extended word-of-mouth and social marketing reach on behalf of producers.

Affective labour – Players consistently discussed social relationships developed through playing ARGs:

> *The cohesion here is amazing, people are generous and kind . . . with a common ends in mind, I don't think there's anything an intelligent, cohesive group of strangers can't do.*
>
> (UF)

Since ARGs require collaborative effort, the community must work together to find clues, solve puzzles, and work through speculations. Individual emotional labour goes into developing what are often akin to working (as well as personal) relationships with other players and understanding their various roles in the game.

User data – Andrejevic (2009) suggests user-created data rather than content is the work product extracted from internet users and commodified under the conditions of private ownership. All the above activities could produce valuable user data for marketers. However, this did not seem to be a primary concern in 2001. Email addresses were collected to contact players, but PMs on The Beast kept no records of player demographics (Lee 2002). The games used standard digital media metrics to gauge success in terms of traffic to and time spent on in-game sites, numbers of players on forums, and so forth. As social media became more prominent, those metrics also became useful, for example, tweets, retweets, likes, and so on. The only way to monitor attitudes towards ARGs was to follow forum discussions, and none of those spaces were owned or controlled by corporate media conglomerates or game producers. So, while this is an aspect of digital labour, it was less relevant for promotional ARG players.

Terranova argues this kind of labour is 'free' in two respects: it is unpaid, but also freely and willingly given. Thus, free labour does not automatically mean exploitation. Several players acknowledged their role as 'marketing tools':

> *Movies are bigger than ever because of the internet. It's turned us fans into cheap marketing tools to spread the buzz.*
>
> (SHH)

> *We're doing the marketing FOR them by dressing up as Jokers and running around and taking pictures. And then one day when they see trailer and other marketing they'll remember us as clowns acting a*

fool and they'll talk about it someone. Which means word of mouth will spread.

(SHH)

This is not unwitting collusion, but nor do these quotes demonstrate resistant behaviour. These players fully understand their position in the system of consumer capitalism. Yet if they perceive this as exploitation and manipulation, why do they continue to play? Janes (2015) outlines several mechanisms by which players can distance themselves from (but not completely disavow) the commercial purpose of promotional ARGs. Arguably, if players position the games as something other than marketing, their work can be understood as something other than marketing labour. Indeed, the TINAG philosophy provides an in-built mechanism for this:

Maintenance of TINAG helps me connect with the product in a way where I don't feel like [I'm being] used.

(Survey Respondent #15)

It's what makes the difference between an ARG and an advertisement.

(Survey Respondent #26)

This is also reflected in Stewart's assertion that 'there is no viral marketing, all there is, is fun' (cited in Hanas 2006). As marketing work became more explicit, the games became more open to criticism because if all there is is viral marketing, the fun is lost:

All the clues they give us are all about the movie. The clips are found in the ads for the movie. It's just like we are the global advertising network for the movie.

(UF)

With Super 8 it ultimately felt like we were being force-fed information and promo materials.

(Survey Respondent #15)

Such tactics remind players that someone is profiting from their suspension of disbelief and making them feel foolish for taking that leap of faith. This tends to be more common in viral campaigns than full-blown ARGs; for example, to receive rewards through the *Fifty Shades of Grey* viral app, players had to frequently tweet, retweet, and share pre-set promotional messages about their involvement with the campaign.

This all makes it look like players, PMs, and the games themselves collude to deny the marketing as much as possible, emphasising the gameful content. Players work for free, everyone endeavours to make it feel like play, and exploitation runs alongside self-exploitation. This might be a fair accusation to level at promotional ARGs, and other forms of branded entertainment. However, the statements above highlight the audience's awareness of the marketing game they are playing. This position is more complicated than complicit/resistant dichotomies allow for, and not a straightforward case of exploitation.

Terranova also notes that 'free labor is the moment where the knowledgeable consumption of culture is translated into productive activities that are pleasurably embraced and at the same time often shamelessly exploited' (2000: 37). She suggests these two things can exist simultaneously, but not unproblematically. Creative labour might not be forcibly taken from ARG players and put to the service of capitalism (which Hesmondhalgh [2010] notes is a requirement for the Marxist definition of exploitation), but it is 'voluntarily channelled and controversially structured within capitalist business practices' (Terranova 2000). Powell (2013) also argues any form of media participation occurs inescapably within a capitalist system, and Hills (2002: 5) similarly suggests fan labour and practices are bound within a consumer capitalist system from which they cannot extract themselves, only learn to live within. Fans occupy a middle ground, whereby they may hold anti-commercial ideologies but continue to display commodity-completist practices. This is a lived contradiction for any fan, so rather than try to close it down, theoretical approaches to fandom must accommodate it.

This is not to suggest players should necessarily be paid for their activities. Indeed, Hesmondhalgh (2010) suggests extending that argument to all unpaid labour in society pushes those activities further into a capitalist system from which we might prefer to keep them separate. Furthermore, it negates the non-financial, positive rewards valued by those involved in that cultural production. Some players expressed concerns about '*being manipulated by the marketing department of Spielberg*' (CM). But they also reflected on how personally rewarding the games were, how they conceived of their participation and its value, and what they felt to be fair 'compensation' for their time and energy. Attending to these expressions might provide what Hesmondhalgh (2010: 280) calls for in terms of a more 'coherent and pragmatic analysis of political struggle and of lived experience'. Closer analysis of forum discussion demonstrates how players understand the value of their own marketing labour and whether they perceive this as 'exploitation'.

'Dreamworks has GIVEN us a wonderful gift' (CM)

Some players viewed promotional ARGs as a 'gift' or 'treat' for fans, reflecting McGonigal's description of promotional ARGs as 'gift marketing' (cited in Economist 2009):

> *All this Joker Marketing stuff feels very much like a gift from WB and Nolan to us.*

(SHH)

From one perspective this negates any need to view players' involvement with the games as labour at all. However, Terranova (2000) warns against this. She takes issue with Barbrook's (1998) definition of the digital economy as being a combination of public, market-driven, and gift economies, arguing he is overly optimistic about the level at which the 'high-tech gift economy' is independent from capitalism:

> It is important to remember that the gift economy, as a part of a larger digital economy, is itself an important force within the reproduction of the labor force in late capitalism as a whole.

(2000: 36)

Whilst Barbrook suggests the gift economy is a way of overcoming capitalist elements in the digital economy, Terranova counters that these forms of production are part of the process by which late capitalism seeks to create monetary value from 'knowledge/culture/affect' (2000: 38). This is not necessarily a negative prospect, but Terranova rightly challenges the somewhat utopian arguments around the emancipatory potentials of the digital economy. She feels such cultural flows within a gifting economy are 'originating within a field that is always and already capitalism' (2000: 38), rather than a means of escaping it. This relates mostly to labour 'gifted' between internet users, or from users to businesses, for example, video game modders or open source software developers. Since it is always already involved in capitalist structures, that labour is not so much appropriated or incorporated but 'channelled'.

In promotional ARGs this is reversed. The 'gift' is the game itself, offered by media companies to fan communities in return for their participation/labour. This terminology is significant because the construction and maintenance of fan communities themselves is also described as being based on a 'gift economy'. Hellekson (2009) explains how fan-produced objects are exchanged within communities based on three elements of 'gifting' identified by Mauss (1990): giving, receiving, and reciprocating. Such objects include fan fiction, art or vids, analysis, discussion, links, GIFs, memes, wiki databases, and conferences. These can be individual gifts from one fan to another, but, as Turk (2014) notes, they are more often received by the community as a whole and may be produced collaboratively. This gift economy can be viewed as a defence from legal action, since no profit is gained from using the IP. It also functions to strengthen the bonds of the community as 'economic investment gives way to sentimental investment' (Jenkins et al. 2013). However, when a corporate media producer enters into this gifting economy, concerns are raised about its appropriation for purely economic gain. The attempts of FanLib.com to profit from fan fiction are often cited as an example of the failure of that enterprise.[4]

In perceiving promotional ARGs as 'gifts' from producers, players can remove themselves from the sphere of commercial economics and place themselves within this fannish gift economy. In Mauss' terms, if producers perform the 'giving' of an ARG, players perform the 'receiving'. Reciprocation is more complicated. Time and energy expended by PMs equates to 'efforts of time and skill' (Hellekson 2009) valued by fan communities. One 'effort gift' from the media company deserves another in return. However, the ARG/gift *requires* that reciprocation to function (there is no game without players), and that fan labour goes on to profit the company in the form of free word-of-mouth marketing. In addition, Scott (2009) argues ancillary content like promotional ARGs are in fact false gifts. They simply 'regift' an acceptable version of fans' own activities back to communities, breaking with the moral economy of gifting and presenting something old as something new. This old/new metaphor works in some respects for promotional ARGs. Asking fans to submit photos of themselves in Joker make-up might be considered a false 'regifting' of existing fan activities like cosplay, but on Warner Bros. terms. There are more, unspoken strings attached to this gift than the expectation of reciprocation – those reciprocal efforts must not threaten Warner Bros.' intellectual property.

Players were suspicious of such 'gifts' due to their perception of media companies as profit-focussed. Instead of participating on the terms of a gift economy in which they feared exploitation, some adopted a more transactional attitude, in tune with a commodity economy. They took a demanding stance, expecting a suitable return on their investment. Many communications during WhySoSerious addressed 42 Entertainment as a customer services outlet, to whom players could direct complaints about faulty products. SHH players seemed most comfortable with this approach, demonstrated when the segment of the game sponsored by Domino's Pizza went awry and some players did not receive the in-game code with their free pizza:

If there is any way that this code could still be received, that is all we are looking for at this point. I don't want a pizza because, honestly,

I don't like Domino's. However, I was willing to have it for dinner seeing that I was about to enjoy something better on line. Please let me know if you have any other information about this. Thanks for your time in reading. Sincerely, Elizabeth and Timothy.

(SHH)

This attitude is possibly more apparent here because the notion of gift-giving relies on a sense of trust which did not necessarily exist between Batman fans and Warner Bros. in 2008. Previous marketing strategies were heavily reliant on merchandise and sponsorship, an overly commercial approach which many fans felt cheapened the franchise. They were therefore suspicious that this campaign might be headed the same way:

Does anyone else feel it's a bit off to advertise the Dark Knight for Dominoes and have toys in cereal boxes. This isn't Batman Forever.

(SHH)

This did not prevent them from acknowledging their role as unpaid marketers, but many seemed to feel the best way to negotiate this system was to play by its rules. They treated the game more like a commercial transaction in which they were a customer than as a gift which might make them appear to have done the work for nothing.

Booth (2010) argues an ARG is an 'amalgam of the gift and the commodity economies', which he refers to as the 'Digi-Gratis' economy. Here the two are mutually beneficial, and one need not necessarily supersede the other. Terranova (2000) might suggest this remains problematic, but by drawing upon notions of both gift and commodity economies, players may manoeuvre themselves into a more comfortable relationship with promotional ARGs in which they stand to benefit from the fruits of their labour as much as producers.

Exchange versus use value – swag

Since even the gifting economy of promotional ARGs cannot be separated from systems of consumer capitalism, we might also turn to Hills' (2002) reading of Adorno to understand how players might resist, without ever truly escaping, that system. Adorno's perspective on mass culture is often considered pessimistic, denying audiences any form of agency within the culture industry. Hills argues there is room for optimism in this work, particularly when it moves away from broader Marxist theory and towards specific instances of consumption. Adorno claims that through play, a child can 'deprive the things with which he plays of their mediated usefulness . . . rescue in them what is benign towards men and not what subserves the exchange relation that equally deforms men and things' (1978: 228). However, this may only be achieved in play. In reality, the child can never completely remove the exchange value from the object. The two values exist simultaneously and, according to Hills, are inseparable. Based on this interpretation, fan appropriation of a text (like the child playing with a toy) moves it away from exchange value and towards use value, without ever separating the two. Hence fans remain within the system they apparently oppose (Hills 2002: 32). That it is only through play that this continuous negotiation can occur makes it an appropriate lens through which to view the work/play of promotional ARG players, specifically the role and value of swag.

'Swag' refers to physical items collected or earned throughout the game. Some ARGs provide more swag than others, and surveyed players actually rated this the least important element of the game.[5] However, analysis of forum discussion suggests this attitude varies between individuals and player communities. Preview screenings were highly prized by WhySoSerious players, whereas Stewart (2012) recalls 'eyerolling' at the notion at the end of The Beast. Cloudmakers were excited to receive movie posters, but swag was never intrinsic to their game. In contrast, WhySoSerious players on Superherohype.com were extremely focussed on receiving any kind of memorabilia. When one player posed the question of what the final in-game reward should be, swag was a popular request:

> *One word. SWAG. Glorious Glorious Swag for everyone. Joker masks, makeup paint, lots more stuff. thats an easy way to make alot of people happy.*
>
> (SHH)

Many felt this was the reward they deserved for the time and effort invested in the game. Several considered it a form of payment, frequently using the term 'payoff'. There were also discussions about the appropriate payoff proportionate to the time invested. Where there were negative evaluations of WhySoSerious, these were usually related to the lack of payoff, almost always measured in terms of swag or exclusive footage. Some responses were more measured than others:

> *The idea and original games were great, and the rewards were proportionate to the tasks (Send some E-mails, clear a picture. But as the campaign has moved on the game have become more tiresome and involve much more hard work and time, which cannot be give up likely – time*

is precious . . . only getting one image for running all over the country isn't an equal deal.

(SHH)

At first, it was really cool. But now. I'm just tired of all the games, and all the waiting. I know some people got Make-Up and Gotham Times and Masks and Wizard World Footage, but you know what? A LOT of other people didn't get jack ****, ****. I'm one of the people who didn't get ****. SO, it's like, HELLO! Where's my slice? I want more than equal rights! I want EVERYTHING FOR FREE!!!

(SHH)

Here, swag is not a gift but appropriate recompense for work undertaken. We can see how Jenkins' (2006) argument for a more demanding audience might be validated here. However, it also highlights that the 'payoff' wasn't equal for every individual, which reinforced community hierarchies. This was particularly evident when swag allocated to a minority gave them access to ARG information earlier than others, for example, Joker Phones.

Rather than physical rewards, some players hoped for documentation of their participation:

On the Dark Knight DVD & Blu-Ray, there will be this big behind the scene feature about the whole 42 Entertainment viral game with a listing congratulation of everyone that was involved.

(SHH)

Here, formal recognition is the substitute for payment or swag. Having been invited to play, players felt producers should make efforts to acknowledge them as a valued part of the process. A similar concern for fair recompense lies beneath the apparently materialistic demand for swag.

Some eschewed this attitude entirely, suggesting the reward was 'the experience itself', or viewing swag as a memento:

I don't think the final prize is [the] *point – it's about getting some neat background info and immersing fans into the world of TDK.*

(SHH)

It represents all this time I spent going nutso over something and I can always look at it and be like, 'Oh yeah . . . that was pretty awesome'.

(SHH)

I plan on passing it along to my son when he gets old enough.

(SHH)

These affective investments can elevate ARGs on Grossberg's 'mattering map', to the point that they become 'places at which we can construct our own identity as something to be invested in, as something that matters' (1992: 57). Swag is important not because it has exchange value, but because it has affective value, relevant to players' personal experiences. Some players were even condemned as being overly materialistic for selling swag online. It was more acceptable to exchange swag internally, with values based on scarcity:

Thou shalt never contribute to people hocking previous viral swag for gregarious prices on ebay. Capitalism. Don't you just loathe it?! People making money from nothing. Swag that was for REAL fans.

(SHH)

No real fan would EVER immediately try to sell [swag] *on ebay.*

(SHH)

I really do like the economy in these forums though – trading swag for swag you missed out on is nice.

(SHH)

This approach reflects Hill's argument that the exchange value of fan objects is not determined by the 'economy proper' in the Marxist sense, but through a 'process of localised (fan-based) use-valuations' (2002: 35). This pulls the object back towards use value and, although it might eventually return to exchange value through the system of consumer capitalism, it does so through processes which are 'underpinned' by the lived experience of fandom (Hills 2002: 35). This is further complicated because promotional ARGs position that 'lived experience' of fandom as something itself imbued with exchange value. For players to rework that exchange value, they would have to actively re-appropriate the value of fan activity itself, and thus the value of the community and its practices. We may have to concede, as Hills (2002) advises, that players cannot be extricated from that economic system. Use and exchange value cannot be fully separated, but at least in this configuration it is not a process over which fans have no influence. By demanding swag and then defining its value through their own systems and moral codes, they are also defining the terms and value of their participation in the game and the value of their labour. On the surface they appear to be working for free, but the complexity of these negotiations in practice means we cannot claim a simple abuse of power or exploitation on the part of media companies producing promotional ARGs.

Relationship marketing – players, PMs, and media companies

The notion of player-defined 'use' overriding corporate-defined 'exchange' value returns us to relationship marketing (RM). The emphasis on the audience as 'co-creator of value' (Vargo & Lusch 2006) is also a key trait of RM. But 'value' need not be solely found in the co-construction of the text itself. Players ascribe their own meanings and values to ARGs, which are often personal and subjective. These do not necessarily correlate with intended uses, meanings, or values denoted by media companies. Kerrigan notes that marketing theory has been moving in this direction for some time, placing more emphasis on the consumer's perceptions of value than those of the producer (2010: 5). ARGs might be considered a further expression of this tendency as media companies take more interest in how audiences create meaning and value in their relationships with media products. This sounds like a positive step, but fears of producers taking those fan-created values and using them for their own financial gain are still valid. This threatens the trust-based relationship RM is seeking to build. Gummesson (1997) argues the ethics of RM (trust, honesty, win-win relationship) are sometimes offered to customers when producers have no real intentions of forging such relationships in practice. Promotional ARGs may be guilty of promising a kind of participation which does not materialise, manipulating fans' emotional investments or using them as free labour to spread positive word of mouth. In this sense, there is an exploitation of the relationships involved in RM, which is fundamentally dishonest.

However, there are two distinct producer/consumer relationships at play here: players/PMs and players/media companies. The diagram in Figure 4.1 highlights mutual dependencies as well as perceptions of conflict in each relationship.

The two function very differently, almost in opposition to each other. In fact, it is not media companies who are engaging in that relationship at all. They maintain a distance from audiences and displace that potential relationship almost fully onto ARG producers like 42 Entertainment. Some players expressed scepticism about the involvement of large media corporations, and several Cloudmakers were initially wary of Microsoft's role in The Beast:

> *Keep in mind Microsoft itself is behind this. When was the last time they were convinced to do anything that wasn't in their best financial interests?*

(CM)

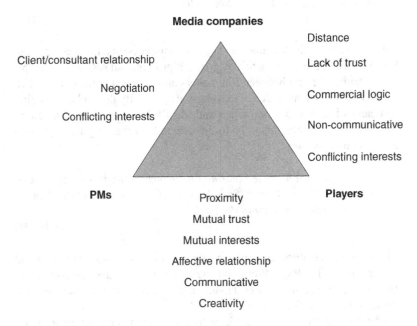

Media companies

Distance

Client/consultant relationship

Lack of trust

Negotiation

Commercial logic

Conflicting interests

Non-communicative

Conflicting interests

PMs

Proximity

Players

Mutual trust

Mutual interests

Affective relationship

Communicative

Creativity

Figure 4.1 Player/PM/media company relationships

However, by the end of the game some attitudes had shifted:

> *I've never had a lot of reason to be charitable to Microsoft. Now, knowing they're cool enough to employ Elan Lee, I'm a *lot* more likely to think well of them.*

> (CM)

Similarly, some WhySoSerious players remained unconvinced that Warner Bros. had any vested interest in the games beyond financial benefits:

> *I don't think that some WB executive woke up one day with a vision that he had to tell the world a special story in a special way, and to hell with what anyone else says he is going to tell the story how it needs to be told because he owes it to the fans and damn the cost/ benefit ratios.*

> (WB)

Yet when the game was over, the conglomerate was frequently congratulated in the same sentence as 42E:

Well done 42E and WB. It's been a blast.

(SHH)

Aligning the two in this manner suggests media companies benefit from RM, but essentially achieve this by proxy. If promotional ARGs are attempting to bridge the gap between filmmakers and audiences (Kerrigan 2010), they use a middleman to do so. Players swiftly identify this, acknowledging companies like 42E as contractors and identifying with them as an entity which is, to an extent, beholden to the demands of that larger company in the same way they are:

> *42E is not completely in control of their own game. Warner Bros commissioned them; Warner Bros is their client, and therefore, Warner Bros can tell them what to do.*

(SHH)

This puts further distance between themselves and media companies and aligns them with PMs. From this perspective, if media companies are attempting to exploit the free labour of audiences via RM, they are not doing so successfully.

Players and PMs further reinforce this distance by defining themselves, their work, and their values against those of corporate clients. They share ethical perspectives regarding the way ARGs are played, which translates into a clearly expressed concern on the part of PMs not to do anything that would exploit players' investments in the games:

> Because there is that *passion*, I will work till midnight to do something that I am paid to do and want to do really well, and I'll work till 2 or 3am because I don't want to let these people down. The amount of energy and passion that the audience puts into these things just seems like it would be a *betrayal*. . . . I am so much more careful about this audience than I am even for the audience for my novels. I try really hard when I'm writing books but I do not feel the same intense *obligation* not to let the audience down that I do with an ARG. And I think I speak for most of us when I say that we cannot let people spend 30 hours a week trying to decode cereal boxes and not really work hard.

(Stewart 2007)

There is a deep sense of mutual respect for labour here. Stewart explicitly notes he is being paid for his time, which implicitly recognises player input as unpaid. Terms like 'passion', 'betrayal', and 'obligation' place emotional and moral value on his labour. Players therefore genuinely feel '*PMs care about their players'* (Survey Respondent #18). By contrast, both players and PMs feel media companies lack this concern, prioritising ends over means:

> *Hollywood will pick money over art any day.*
>
> (CM)

> I think media companies only care in so much as it works. Whereas I think 42 or Fourth Wall would say we would prefer not to do something that exploits players, even if it works in potentially selling tickets or making money.
>
> (Hon 2012)

Stewart (2012) also described the experience of trying to meet player expectations, despite this becoming increasingly difficult, time consuming, and a little soul destroying:

> It's very, very difficult to sustain making gigantic amounts of new content on the fly, reactively, for months. We tried to build something that didn't require that with ilovebees, where you could put more of it in the can in advance so you weren't working 20hr days for 6 months. 3 weeks in people just hated that, they want you to respond . . . part of it is expectations, they knew we were doing it, and they were expecting to have that experience, and they weren't getting that experience and the thing wasn't responsive enough for them. So I won't say we wept like little children but it was pretty close, when we made the decision, we just have to, have to increase that level of engagement. And you're sitting there saying we can't, we can't, we can't, we've got 9 weeks left to go, if we start tap dancing now, not only is it going to have to be tap dancing, it's got to get more extreme. And we have to do more every week because that's the build, that's the promise you're making.

For their part, players were keen to ensure games were played in a manner which respected PM's efforts, for example, not brute forcing passwords:

> Stewart – We assumed guns blazing, and were actually very struck by the intense ethicality of a lot of the players.
> Player – I always felt guilty that we brute-forced Rational Hatter.
>
> (Cloudmakers 2001)

We have been blessed by a consensual, shared immersive environment they [PMs] have painstakingly and expensively put together. Rather than half-assing it and just going with whatever they scripted no matter how quickly we blew through it, they have constantly adapted to our techniques, our skills, our knowledge and likely to our theories. They have given us the product of their sweat, their labor, their creativity, their muses, their passion and their skill, without even the ability to have their e-mail addresses attached so we can send them mail and say 'this is really really good'.

(CM)

Players certainly identified shared experiences with PMs. The sleepless nights, long hours, and emotional investments position both parties as being involved in a 'labour of love'. This is identified by Friedson (1990) and subsequently discussed by Hesmondhalgh (2013: 255) and McRobbie (2015) as a common phenomenon which explains a tendency towards self-exploitation in the creative industries. One anecdote highlights the easily blurred boundaries between personal and private life for those running an ARG, and the technological and logistical perils of producing something like this in real time:

We totally broke their servers on multiple occasions. During Operation Slipknot, the phone server . . . completely fizzled and they decided to divert it to Twitchy's [PM pseudonym] personal phone while they tried to fix it. His voicemail immediately filled up and players started getting his phone number on his voicemail message and apparently it was posted here. Twitchy still gets spam calls to this day.

(SHH)

Players expressed their appreciation for producers' work, ranging from thank you messages on forums to tribute websites and bespoke videos. Some suggested providing feedback in a format 42 Entertainment could present to future clients. This acknowledgement of the corporate side of the company was not unusual, but an affection and a human connection remained:

This is also for the individual 42e employee, the guy and gal like you 'n me who worked long hours, busted their butt . . . and every night when they went to sleep they were wondering what would come of their hard work. . . . If you want to spend the time to create a business presentation explaining our thanks to give to the higher ups @ WB, please . . . do . . . they'll need it. but 42e & DC are human companies. not mindless corporate machines.

(SHH)

This configuration makes it harder to accuse PMs of outright exploitation but does almost work to justify the free labour of player communities by making them comparable to the paid labour of game designers.

Both parties also understand that labour to be predominately creative, rather than commercial. Christiano (2013) specifically identifies himself as a creative first, businessman second. Others describe their work as 'ARG for ARG's sake. Kind of a pun on "art for art's sake"' (Brackin 2007). Players often shared this position:

This is not a game . . . it's art.

(CM)

Even though this is all just marketing, I like to think 42 sees it as more than that.

(SHH)

Do you honestly think, given the amounts of creativity they've displayed in their efforts, that they are looking at this as 'just another job'?

(CM)

In contrast, PMs discussed the difficulties of convincing corporate clients of the value of ARGs beyond digital marketing metrics. Unlike standardised measurements like Nielsen ratings for TV, these are many and varied, making it hard to convey success to a client who might 'start comparing apples to oranges a little and say "Well, you're not getting the World of Warcraft figures that we were thinking"' (Brackin 2007). Six years on from The Beast, Lee felt the industry still lacked an understanding of what ARGs were and where they belonged:

> They're not sure, are we part of marketing, are we a standalone project? We get a tiny percent of the ad-spend because they try to shoehorn us into this bizarre-shaped box where 'Hey that's how much it costs to build a website, so take it and build a website, call it an ARG and we're done'.
>
> (Lee 2007)

PMs recognised the need to appeal to the full spectrum of players, but felt corporate clients weren't interested in reaching the core player community (who do much of the work), but in the wider audience (Clark 2007). This suggests clients may not appreciate the importance of the free labour provided by those core players. PMs, on the other hand, frequently extol the value of those players:

> The game isn't the art, or the puzzles or the story. . . . They are designed to precipitate, to catalyse the actual work of art. Which is YOU.
>
> (Stewart cited in McGonigal 2008: 203)

The implication here is that players and PMs have a shared understanding of an ARG's value and the labour involved that corporate clients do not. Players align themselves with PMs in terms of co-creation of value, as per the principles of relationship marketing (RM). This leads to a sense of a balanced relationship, but if that relationship becomes distant, players can feel used, or taken for granted. Surveyed players noted a shift in the kind of engagement they had with PMs on promotional games:

> *These days a movie promotional game is rarely a true ARG in the traditional sense, and the relationship to the audience differs from the kind of engagement players feel with smaller ARGs run for the sake of its own story-telling model.*

(Survey Respondent #8)

As the player/PM relationship becomes less responsive, players may lose that sense of trust. If the game requires them to communicate with it, they want it to talk back. Even in games where that connection was missing, players continued to appeal to PMs directly:

> *Pssst, if you're reading this Super 8 viral people – THROW US A BONE!*

(UF)

To reduce this potential for dialogue to one-way traffic removes a key appeal of ARGs, confounds player expectations, and prevents it from working as RM. As the level of watching and monitoring (which provides key metrics for evaluating the campaign) starts to outweigh the level of responding and modifying (which isn't strictly necessary to get those measures of success), the communication channel becomes narrower. Players are less likely to feel 'heard' in the game in the way Stewart (2012) promotes, and more likely to feel exploited. One survey respondent refers to the importance of being valued as a contributor to a marketing exercise rather than '*one of many sheep in marketing campaign*' (Survey Respondent #15), herded through an experience in which they played no meaningful part. Moreover, the lack of trust means players are less likely to feel comfortable making the affective investments that lead to the empowering experiences detailed in Chapter 3.

Conclusion

We can make links between the activity undertaken in playing a promotional ARG and what Terranova (2000) describes as 'free labour' in the sense of digital marketing work. The games require the construction and maintenance of forums, wikis, and other forms of UGC, both 'official' and 'unofficial'. ARGs require 'work-as-play' in the form of puzzle solving, narrative speculation, chat, and affective labour to form cohesive player communities. This labour is indeed 'freely and willingly given' (Terranova 2000), but since it eventually benefits media companies as a form of unpaid marketing work, it seems easy to accuse media companies of exploiting audiences' investments of time, emotion, and energy for their own commercial gain.

Looking closely at how players themselves perceive this situation reveals a more complex situation. Whilst clearly aware of their role in marketing campaigns, players had various ways of negotiating that position within a consumer capitalist system. Viewing the games as part of a 'gift economy' was one tactic which allowed them to distance themselves from that system, although it was still problematic given that the gift came with significant strings attached. Alternatively, some players took a more transactional attitude to their role. If they felt they were not being adequately recompensed for their work, they approached game producers accordingly as customers who had paid for something in time and energy but were not receiving the appropriate 'payoff'. This does not remove them from the commodity economy – indeed, that is impossible. Instead it leaves them working within what Booth calls the Digi-Gratis economy (2010), which allows them to demand the fruits of their labour. That could simply be a positive game experience but was often linked specifically to swag. Players then define the value of those items within their own systems, rather than those of the economy proper, much as Hills argues fan communities use 'localised (fan-based) use-valuations' (2002: 35). Again, they cannot remove themselves, the ARGs, or their labour from these economic systems, but they can participate in them on their own terms. The sense in which this work is then being 'exploited' is therefore more carefully negotiated than it first appears.

Finally, it might seem media companies are exploiting players in that they are seeking to use relationship marketing techniques and values (trust, honesty, win-win relationship) which the games have no capability or intention of providing. However, this situation is complicated by the fact that there are two producer/consumer relationships at play. When media companies hire specialists like 42 Entertainment, they displace that relationship, distancing themselves from audiences rather than using relationship marketing to bridge that gap. They might reap some benefits by proxy, but ultimately the trusting, co-creative relationship occurs between players and PMs. Both parties reinforce that distance by defining themselves strongly against the corporate client and aligning themselves as co-creators of value in a way which avoids the feeling of exploitation. However, if that relationship deteriorates or becomes more distant (thus moving closer to that of the media company), the trust is lost, and players may indeed start to feel exploited or taken for granted. The notion of labour exploitation in an ARG is clearly not straightforward, and ultimately the genre opens up more possibilities for different configurations of producer/consumer relationships that do not conform neatly to binary notions of exploitation and collaborative co-creation. This may provide alternative frameworks for examining these relationships in the future as participatory marketing continues to ask consumers to invest their time and energy in promotional experiences.

Notes

1 www.unfiction.com/about/support-uf/
  Closure of the forums is in part due to changes in the founder's personal financial situation.
2 Wikis for Super 8 http://super8.wikibruce.com/Home and WhySoSerious http://batman.wikibruce.com/Whysoserious.com
3 www.whysoseriousredux.com
4 FanLib's approach was flawed because it failed to recognise the nature of the community it was attempting to co-opt and its status as a pre-existing community, as opposed to a community created and controlled by FanLib itself (Jenkins 2007; de Kosnik 2009; Hellekson 2009).
5 Players were asked to rate six key elements of the games according to their importance. On average players felt strong storytelling was most important, followed (in descending order) by engaging characterisation, challenging puzzles, a large and active player community, real-life meet-ups and games, the opportunity to acquire swag.

References

Adorno, T. W. (1978) *Minima Moralia: Reflections from Damaged Life*, London: Verso.
Andrejevic, M. (2008) 'Watching Television Without Pity: The Productivity of Online Fans', *Television & New Media*, 9(1), pp. 24–46.
Andrejevic, M. (2009) 'Exploiting YouTube: Contradictions of User-Generated Labour', in P. Snickers & P. Vonderau, eds., *The YouTube Reader*. Stockholm: National Library of Sweden.
Bakioğlu, B. (2018) 'Exposing Convergence: YouTube, Fan Labour, and Anxiety of Cultural Production in Lonelygirl15', *Convergence: The International Journal of Research into New Media Technologies*, 24(2), pp. 184–204.
Barbrook, R. (1998) 'The High-Tech Gift Economy', *First Monday*, 3(12), 07.12.1998.
Booth, P. (2010) *Digital Fandom*, New York, NY; Oxford: Peter Lang.
Brackin, A. L. (2007) *ARGFest Transcript 03 – Panel 1 – Developing an ARG*. Available: https://web.archive.org/web/20080331221502/http://wiki.argfestocon.com/index.php?title=2007vt03_Transcription [Accessed 04.01.2019].
Chin, B. (2014) 'Sherlockology and Galactica.tv: Fan Sites as Gifts or Exploited Labor?' *Transformative Works and Cultures*, (15).
Christiano, J. (2013) *Email Interview with Author*, 06.03.2013.

Clark, B. (2007*) ARGFest Transcript 03 – Panel 1 – Developing an ARG*. Available: https://web.archive.org/web/20080331221502/http://wiki.argfestocon.com/index.php?title=2007vt03_Transcription [Accessed 05.01.2019].

Cloudmakers. (2001) *Post-Game Puppetmaster Chat*, 31.07.2001. Available: http://groups.yahoo.com/neo/groups/cloudmakers/files [Accessed 11.01.2019].

De Kosnik, A. (2009) 'Should fan fiction be free?', *Cinema Journal*, 48:4, pp. 118–124.

de Kosnik, A. (2013) 'Fandom as Free Labour', in T. Scholz, ed., *Digital Labor the Internet as Playground and Factory*, London: Routledge.

The Economist. (2009) 'Serious Fun', *The Economist Historical Archive, 1843–2010*, (8621), p. 13, 07.03.2009.

Friedson, E. (1990) 'Labors of Love: A Prospectus', in K. Erikson & S. P. Vallas, eds., *The Nature of Work*, New Haven, CT: Yale University Press, pp. 149–161.

Grossberg, L. (1992) 'Is There a Fan in the House? The Affective Sensibility of Fandom', in L. A. Lewis, ed., *The Adoring Audience*, London: Routledge, pp. 50–68.

Gummesson, E. (1997) 'Relationship Marketing as a Paradigm Shift: Some Conclusions from the 30R Approach', *Management Decision*, 35(4), pp. 267–272.

Hanas, J. (2006) 'Games People Play', *Creativity*, 14(1), p. 14, January.

Hellekson, K. (2009) 'A Fannish Field of Value: Online Fan Gift Culture', *Cinema Journal*, 48(4), pp. 118–124.

Hesmondhalgh, D. (2010) 'User-Generated Content, Free Labour and the Cultural Industries', *Ephemera: Theory & Politics in Organization* 10(3–4), pp. 267–284.

Hesmondhalgh, D. (2013) *The Cultural Industries*, 3rd Edition, London: Sage.

Hills, M. (2002) *Fan Cultures*, London; New York, NY: Routledge.

Hon, A. (2012) *Interview with Author*, 26.10.2012, London.

Janes, S. (2015) 'Promotional Alternate Reality Games – More Than "Just" Marketing', *Arts and the Market Special Issue: Teasers Titles and Trailers*, 5(2).

Jenkins, H. (2006) *Convergence Culture: Where Old and New Media Collide*, New York, NY; London: New York University Press.

Jenkins, H. (2007) *Transforming Fan Culture into User-Generated Content: The Case of FanLib*, 22.02.2007. Available: www.henryjenkins.org/2007/05/transforming_fan_culture_into.html [Accessed 04.01.2015].

Jenkins, H., Ford, S. & Green, J. (2013) *Spreadable Media: Creating Value and Meaning in a Networked Culture*, New York, NY: New York University Press.

Kerrigan, F. (2010) *Film Marketing*, Amsterdam; Boston; London: Elsevier, Butterworth-Heinemann.

Lee, E. (2002) *This Is Not a Game: A Discussion of the Creation of the AI Web Experience*, Game Developers Conference, San Jose, CA., 22.03.2002. Available: http://groups.yahoo.com/neo/groups/cloudmakers/files [Accessed 11.01.2019].

Lee, E. (2007) *ARGFest Transcript 05 – Roundtable – 42 Entertainment – Development Process*. Available: http://wiki.argfestocon.com/index.php?title=2007vt05_Transcription&action=edit [Accessed 17.01.2019].

Mauss, M. (1990) *The Gift: The Form and Reason for Exchange in Archaic Societies*, London: Routledge.

McGonigal, J. (2008) 'Why I Love Bees: A Case Study in Collective Intelligence Gaming', in K. Salen, ed., *The Ecology of Games*, Cambridge, MA; London: MIT Press, pp. 199–227.

McRobbie, A. (2015) *Be Creative: Making a Living in the New Culture Industries,* Cambridge: Polity Press.

Powell, H., ed. (2013) *Promotional Culture and Convergence: Markets, Methods, Media,* London; New York, NY: Routledge.

Puppetmaster FAQ. (2001) Available: http://web.archive.org/web/20020810185009/http://familiasalla-es.cloudmakers.org:80/credits/note/faq.html [Accessed 11.01.2019].

Scholz, T., ed. (2013) *Digital Labor the Internet as Playground and Factory,* London: Routledge.

Scott, S. (2009) 'Repackaging Fan Culture: The Regifting Economy of Ancillary Content Models', *Transformative Works and Cultures,* 3. Available: http://journal.transformativeworks.org/index.php/twc/article/view/150/122 [Accessed 17.01.2019].

Stewart, S. (2007) *ARGFest Transcript 05 – Roundtable – 42 Entertainment – Development Process.* Available: http://wiki.argfestocon.com/index.php?title=2007vt05_Transcription&action=edit [Accessed 11.01.2019].

Stewart, S. (2012) *Interview with Author,* 10–12.2012, London.

Terranova, T. (2000) 'Free Labor: Producing Culture for the Digital Economy', *Social Text,* 63, 18(2), pp. 33–58.

Turk, T. (2014) 'Fan Work: Labor, Worth, and Participation in Fandom's Gift Economy', *Transformative Works and Cultures,* 15. Available: http://journal.transformativeworks.org/index.php/twc/article/view/518/428 [Accessed 17.01.2019].

Vargo, S. & Lusch, R. (2006) 'Service-Dominant Logic: What It Is, What It Is Not, What It Might Be', in S. Vargo & R. Lusch, eds., *The Service-Dominant Logic of Marketing,* Armonk, NY: M.E. Sharpe.

Conclusion

ARGs are a remarkably unique genre of digital storytelling, yet difficult to define. The genre itself is relatively fluid and bears similarities to several other modes of digital storytelling. In a world where virtual, augmented, mixed, and alternative realities are all in play, it can be unclear where ARGs fit in. Their blurring of the boundaries between text/promotion, fiction/ reality, and online/offline engagement makes it difficult to pinpoint a fixed definition of ARGs. As pieces of marketing, they draw upon strategies from viral and immersive marketing to relationship marketing and branded content, making it equally difficult to position them in an industry context.

But it is precisely the ways in which they blur those lines that makes them fascinating sites to investigate relationships between media producers and consumers, examining how those unique dynamics might bring us to more nuanced understandings of power in the contemporary media landscape. Sitting at an intriguing intersection between games and play, narrative storytelling and advertising, they offer the opportunity to engage critically with issues of participation, consumer empowerment, and digital labour.

ARGs emerged in the late 1990s/early 2000s amid shifting modes of media consumption and significant technological change. The rise of complex narratives in film and television, coupled with an increased popularity in gaming, paints a picture of an active, inquisitive audience – ready to be challenged by something more complicated than traditional linear storytelling. Simultaneously, marketers were forming new views on the nature of consumers spending increasing amounts of time online, making purchases via the internet and discussing those purchases at length in public forums. They saw a more active, inattentive audience, seeking novel and affecting experiences as much as high-quality products. All these changes indicated a more active mode of media consumption, and some made claims for more empowered consumers (Jenkins 2006). Promotional ARGs appear to uphold those claims, but also reveal a more complex situation.

The development of the genre between 2000 and 2010 saw an evolution into a more stable genre with clearer rules, norms, and structures. However, the complexity of earlier games was reduced to make them more accessible to wider audiences. Puzzles still required the involvement of the hive mind, but those demanding more specialist knowledge were often dropped in favour of more popular live events, password breaking, and code-cracking. Narratives became less convoluted and, in some games, characterisation became less intricate. The relationship between players and PMs also shifted from something close and personal to a more distant mode of engagement. However, the sense of this relationship as co-operative, collaborative, and co-creative was not entirely lost. It is arguable that at this point commercial intent began to override creative content, leading to a reduction in large-scale, complex promotional ARGs and a push towards less interactive viral campaigns that made use of the growing popularity of social media networks like Facebook and Twitter.

However, promotional ARGs had always been labour-intensive, risky prospects and much of the appeal for corporate executives lay in their novelty and apparently low cost in relation to expensive print and broadcast campaigns. Their relationship to viral marketing boosted their reputation as an innovative, creative, cost-effective strategy which relied to a certain extent on the audience to do the marketing work. Yet, their ROI was difficult to prove, measurements for success were varied and vague, and they seemed to speak most strongly to smaller, pre-existing fan audiences. As the 2008 financial crash took its toll on marketing budgets globally, ARGs were less likely to provide the PR column inches they had in their early days and were looking far less attractive. Smaller, purely web-based initiatives that made use of the ready-made audiences on social media networks were cheaper to run and easier to measure using standardized social metrics. It became harder to justify promotional games which ran for months and involved expensive and logistically complex scavenger hunts for small groups of fans, when wider audiences seemed just as happy to interact with a brand or narrative world through measurable likes and shares.

The internal conflict of a promotional ARG was also a time-honoured one between creativity and commerce. As pieces of 'branded entertainment', their dual roles as storytellers and story-sellers sometimes made it difficult to establish their precise purpose in marketing campaigns. Different production contexts mean this is slightly different in each case study discussed here. The Beast was viewed as an experiment – the percentage of the marketing budget executives were willing to allocate to something that did not have proven effectiveness but might be worth the risk given its innovative nature. WhySoSerious was a more commercial endeavour, carefully embedded within the wider campaign and more engaged with corporate sponsors.

It was also heavily tasked with managing audience expectations during the reboot of a franchise with a long history. Super 8's role as marketing was similarly more obvious, but the multi-agency approach meant the relationship between the ARG's various assets was not always clear.

All three case studies demonstrate attempts to capitalise on affective economics (Jenkins 2006) and the 'fanification' (Nikunen 2007) of a mainstream audience to encourage emotional investments in the games and their associated films. They can also be seen as attempts to construct or manage 'brand communities' (Muniz & O'Guinn 2001) and to offer a sense of involvement, participation, and co-ownership of brands. According to some, this is a form of 'brand democracy' (Kiley 2005), with traditionally rigid gatekeepers softening their approach to IP protection in the name of engaging an active audience demanding more opportunities for meaningful participation in media products. For theorists like Jenkins (2006), affective economics should lead to more empowered consumers with more say over the kinds of media products they want to see from producers. It is a small but significant step in gaining greater control over media production. Chapter 3 challenged these assertions by looking more closely at what it really means to participate in a promotional ARG, the kinds of empowerment they might promise, and the lived reality of players who engage with them.

Chapter 3 also notes debates around the 'power' afforded to players to affect the narrative of an ARG (Lee cited in Rose 2007; McGonigal 2008; Smith 2008; Hon 2012). The real-time nature of the games' development means this is not a choose-your-own-adventure-novel kind of choice, but an opportunity to force game producers to make changes to the planned narrative in accordance with the preferences of player communities. In reality, the chances of having this kind of impact are slim-to-none. In many ways the games offer only an illusion of this kind of narrative control. However, this focus on narrative agency negates more complex ways in which players engage with them. It disregards the fact that players are aware of the limitations of their in-game agency and continue to play regardless. Although this is a key element of ARGs' appeal, there are other factors which drive them to play.

On closer inspection of data pulled from forums and surveys, it becomes clear that affective connections are made by players with characters, the communities they play with, and PMs themselves. This 'affective sensibility' allows players to place ARGs on what Grossberg (1992) calls their 'mattering maps'. This provides the potential for personal and emotional empowerment, as well as the possibility of political resistance and popular struggle. This form of empowerment via popular culture is explicitly not the power to control textual production or meaning, but is no less important or influential in the lives of players. This is exemplified in player testimonials expressing a keen belief that the skills developed in-game translate into real-world impact. This could be as dramatic as helping to solve international crimes or as local as developing their people management skills. Furthermore, the status of the text on Grossberg's (1992) 'mattering map' allows players to use ARGs as a locus for their own identities. Relationships and skills developed in the games genuinely allow players to develop their sense of self. None of these outcomes are intended by media companies and allow for a kind of personal empowerment to come from an interaction with marketing materials beyond their somewhat broken promise of textual control. However, these highly emotional investments are still being made in the service of a marketing campaign. This leads us to question whether media companies are exploiting this affective empowerment for their own gain, and whether this negates what players may have achieved personally.

Players effectively perform unpaid marketing work, spreading (mostly positive) word of mouth about the ARG and the media property it promotes. Whilst that work is coded as play, the activities involved in playing a promotional ARG fit the categories described by Terranova (2000) as 'free labour'. These range from forum construction and maintenance, to solving puzzles, participating in online discussions, and generating content that feeds officially or unofficially into the game's narrative. It includes affective and emotional labour as players build and maintain collaborative working relationships throughout campaigns.

Most players seem aware of their role in this arrangement, but closer analysis of survey and forum data reveals a variety of sometimes opposing self-conceptualisations of their work. Nonetheless, these all resist straightforward notions of exploitation or manipulation. One approach considers ARGs as part of a 'gifting' economy rather than a consumer capitalist economy proper. The gift economy is often referred to as one component of the multifaceted digital economy, or in discussions of fan communities (McGonigal cited in Economist 2009; Barbrook 1998; Murdock 2003; Hellekson 2009; Booth 2010; Turk 2014). However, it is still difficult to extricate this gifting economy from capitalist structures entirely (Terranova 2000). When a corporate media producer enters into that economy of gifting, players may become cynical about the legitimacy of the 'gift' (Scott 2009). If media companies are using gifting to profit from players, that gift becomes false, untrustworthy, and undeserving of reciprocation. In this case, players may revert to treating the games in a more transactional, commercial manner. They may address PMs as a company providing them with a product they paid for in their time and energy, and of which they can therefore demand a certain level of quality. This may not remove players from the system of consumer capitalism, but playing by its rules allows them to make demands of producers which a gifting economy cannot.

Since even the gifting economy cannot truly be separated from systems of capitalism, we might look to other elements of ARGs where players indicate how they value their labour in ways other than as marketing work. Swag is often treated in a transactional manner, with players deeming this a 'payoff' for their investments in the games. However, this was not always deemed proportionate to the work completed. One player noted: '*only getting one* [behind-the-scenes] *image for running all over the country isnt an equal deal*' (SHH).

Others requested recognition of their work in the form of acknowledgements in the game, or viewed the game itself as the 'reward' for playing. Moreover, players imbued swag with an affective value beyond a price tag. Most agreed it was inappropriate to sell swag for money and preferred to exchange it within the community for other items missed on the way. This self-defined, affective value system allows them to move the game experience, their labour, and their swag away from the 'economy proper' and closer to what Adorno would call 'use value'. Again, this does not remove them or their work from a system of consumer capitalism, but unlike the transactional approach it lets them participate in this system somewhat on their own terms.

Finally, this value creation returns us to relationship marketing, which emphasises audiences as 'co-creators of value'. That relationship demands a certain level of respect, trust, and honesty; some marketers have been accused of simply paying lip service to, rather than fulfilling, these requirements. It might initially appear that promotional ARGs are guilty of this; however, there are two player/producer relationships here, and each works slightly differently. By hiring a separate company to act as 'middlemen' in the delivery of the games, media companies put further distance between themselves and the audience. Any relationship that develops here is primarily between players and PMs, with media companies tending to benefit by proxy. This distance is reinforced by that player/PM relationship, in which both sides define themselves, their work, and their values strongly against those of the media company they are both effectively working for. Involvement in the games is something of a 'labour of love' for both sides, a position which leaves them both open to the exploitation/self-exploitation of their creative labour (see McRobbie 2015). In some respects, the deeply held respect for player communities expressed by PMs makes it difficult to suggest this relationship is truly being intentionally exploited. On the other hand, this configuration enables players to equate their unpaid labour with the paid marketing work produced by PMs. If this relationship becomes more distant and less responsive, that trust weakens and players are more likely to feel taken advantage of.

As we start to see fewer full-blown ARGs and more lightweight viral campaigns, the 'payoff' decreases and the marketing work becomes more obvious across the experience. In the *Fifty Shades of Grey* campaign, the amount of sharing on social media required to progress the game was not only explicit but was not comparable to the rewards. The first reward was an image of Christian Grey's helicopter and the second a photo of two Grey Enterprises receptionists. Both could have been stock photos as opposed to the actual stills or behind-the-scenes shots fans would have wanted. This does not seem adequate recompense for what is clearly social media marketing work, even accounting for the fact that the effort required to tweet is far less than that of attending a scavenger hunt.

Promotional ARGs bring consumers and producers together in a manner which challenges common perceptions of power in media, and the meaning and value of 'active participation' in a shifting media landscape. It points not to a dissolution of boundaries or reversal of power structures, but a space in which they are continually in flux, and can be understood and valued in different ways. Most striking are the personal, emotional, and subjective experiences of individual ARG players and PMs. The potential of the genre to have this kind of impact is astounding, even considering the commercial context and constraints of a promotional game. This makes them not only fascinating to research, but worthy of respectful and careful attention. The games do make and have made people feel like they have been part of something important, and for some, if only for a short period of time, like superheroes.

Further research may consider aspects of ARGs which have not been explored here. There is more work to be done on the role of gender in player communities and of women in transmedia industries. From an industry perspective, there are a few significant women involved in ARG design and production (e.g. Christy Dena, Andrea Phillips, Jane McGonigal), all of whom have written extensively about their work. The history of male dominance in computer game design, misogyny in gaming culture, and issues around gender representation in games might lead to assumptions that these problems also apply to ARG design and development. A combination of ethnography and textual analysis might shed light on whether these problems are replicated in ARG production and consumption, or whether they might offer women space to develop more diverse stories or forms of representation.

Despite the insistence that the player community is evenly split with regards to gender, this was not the case for surveyed players, and it does not follow that because more women play, their contributions are valued in the same way. However, one player did highlight a specifically gendered angle to her sense of empowerment:

> *I've been playing for a long time (7 years I think). It's been fun being a girl and not being stared at by gawkers just because I actually have a) an opinion and b) can find things no one noticed.*

(UF)

The idea of an ARG (promotional or otherwise) as a safe online space for women would be fruitful to pursue, particularly at a time when so much of the internet appears increasingly hostile towards women. Finally, whilst this book focusses specifically on promotional games, fan-produced and grassroots games deserve equal attention. Örnebring's (2007) comparison between promotional and fan-produced ARGs could be extended to consider their differences, similarities, and reputations within player communities. Stand-alone commercial ARGs are also under-researched, and games like *Ingress* and *Pokémon GO* are blurring the boundaries between alternate and augmented reality gaming as the genre continues to evolve. This may well amount to a different configuration of the producer/consumer relationship than the one depicted here. As one survey respondent cautioned me:

ARGs aren't just advertising campaigns. Keep that in mind.

(Survey Respondent #21)

References

Barbrook, R. (1998) 'The High-Tech Gift Economy', *First Monday*, 3(12).

Booth, P. (2010) *Digital Fandom*, New York, NY; Oxford: Peter Lang.

The Economist. (2009) 'Serious Fun', *The Economist Historical Archive, 1843–2010*, (8621), p. 13, 07.03.2009.

Grossberg, L. (1992) 'Is There a Fan in the House? The Affective Sensibility of Fandom', in L. A. Lewis, ed., *The Adoring Audience*, London: Routledge, pp. 50–68.

Hellekson, K. (2009) 'A Fannish Field of Value: Online Fan Gift Culture', *Cinema Journal*, 48(4), pp. 118–124.

Hon, A. (2012) *Interview with Author*, 26.10.2012, London.

Jenkins, H. (2006) *Convergence Culture: Where Old and New Media Collide*, New York, NY; London: New York University Press.

Kiley, D. (2005) 'Advertising of, by, and for the People', *BusinessWeek*, (3944), pp. 63–64.

McGonigal, J. (2008) 'Why I Love Bees: A Case Study in Collective Intelligence Gaming', in K. Salen, ed., *The Ecology of Games*, Cambridge, MA; London: MIT Press.

McRobbie, A. (2015) *Be Creative: Making a Living in the New Culture Industries*, Cambridge: Polity Press.

Muniz, A. & O'Guinn, T. (2001) 'Brand Community', *Journal of Consumer Research*, 27(4), pp. 412–432.

Murdock, G. (2003) 'Back to Work', in Andrew Beck, ed., *Cultural Work*, London: Routledge.

Nikunen, K. (2007) 'The Intermedial Practices of Fandom', *Nordicom Review*, 28(2), pp. 111–128.

Örnebring, H. (2007) 'Alternate Reality Gaming and Convergence Culture', *International Journal of Cultural Studies*, 10(4), pp. 445–462.

Rose, F. (2007) 'Secret Website, Coded Messages: The New World of Immersive Games', *Wired Magazine*, 16(1). Available: www.wired.com/entertainment/music/magazine/16-01/ff_args [Accessed 11.01.2019].

Scott, S. (2009) 'Repackaging Fan Culture: The Regifting Economy of Ancillary Content Models', *Transformative Works and Cultures*, 3. Available: http://journal.transformativeworks.org/index.php/twc/article/view/150/122 [Accessed 17.01.2019].

Smith, N. (2008) 'Following the Scent', *New Media Age*, pp. 23–24, 9.10.2008.

Terranova, T. (2000) 'Free Labor: Producing Culture for the Digital Economy', *Social Text*, 63, 18(2), pp. 33–58.

Turk, T. (2014) 'Fan Work: Labor, Worth, and Participation in Fandom's Gift Economy', *Transformative Works and Cultures*, 15. Available: http://journal.transformativeworks.org/index.php/twc/article/view/518/428 [Accessed 17.01.2019].

Glossary

For further definitions of ARG-specific terms, see: www.unfiction.com/ glossary/

Alternate reality game (ARG)   Immersive interactive narrative games. The story is revealed through multiple media channels including websites, emails, phone calls, instant messaging, and live and in-person events. In order to further the plot, players must solve puzzles and crack codes. These are typically too complex for one player alone, so they organise into online communities based around forums. These communities share information and speculate on the progress of the game and the possible conclusions.

Augmented reality (AR)   A technology that superimposes a computer-generated image on a user's view of the real world, providing a composite view. AR can be experienced using a smartphone/tablet screen or wearable devices such as connected glasses.

Bad Robot   Film and television production company led by producer and director J.J. Abrams. Originally based at Touchstone Television, it moved to Paramount and Warner Bros. when his own contract with ABC expired. Notable TV series include *Alias, Lost,* and *Westworld.* Feature-length films include *Cloverfield, Super 8,* and reboots of franchises including *Star Trek, Mission: Impossible,* and *Star Wars.*

Brute force   Using a program to bombard a site with scripted input or page requests in order to 'solve' a form-based puzzle or discover hidden directories or pages. This was often frowned upon or considered a form of cheating, since discoveries were not generally designed to be made in this manner.

Massively multiplayer online role-playing games (MMORPGs)   Often seen as a direct descendent of MUDs, these role-playing games are extremely large in scale and involve a persistent online world which continues to run and evolve whilst the player is away from the game. Examples include EverQuest and World of Warcraft.

Microtransactions (also referred to as the 'freemium' model) Video game business model in which in-game purchases are made during a game which is initially free to play. These are often small in terms of value, but players may use them increasingly frequently to progress faster through the game. They are a staple of the mobile gaming market but can also be seen in console and PC games.

Multi-user dungeons (MUDs) Real-time virtual worlds in which players enact role-playing games. These are usually text- or chat-based, as players describe rooms, characters, objects, and actions as the events of the game unfold.

Puppetmasters (PMs) Term used to describe designers running an ARG 'behind the curtain'. Coined by Cloudmakers during The Beast when it was unclear precisely who was behind the game.

Rabbit hole Entry point for any ARG. This is usually a website but can also be found in clues in other more traditional promotional material such as posters and film trailers.

Rocket Poppeteers Fictional ice-lolly brand that forms a key strand in the Super 8 ARG. Listed ingredients include kaitei no mitsu (Seabed's Nectar), an apparently addictive substance which is also an ingredient in fictional drink Slusho.

Sandbox games Video games in which players may roam and explore a vast, open virtual world. They typically have fewer restrictions and higher levels of player autonomy than other, more linear games. Players can often choose which goals and storylines to follow, or reject these entirely and simply explore the terrain on offer with no specific endpoint in mind.

Slusho Fictional beverage brand that appears repeatedly in J.J. Abrams productions, including *Alias*, *Cloverfield*, and *Super 8*.

Swag Free merchandise, objects, and other paraphernalia collected by players during an ARG. This ranges from posters and stickers to t-shirts and mobile phones. Much of this material refers to game-specific events – for example, posters and window stickers to accompany Harvey Dent's political campaign in WhySoSerious.

TINAG/This Is Not A Game A defining but not uncontested philosophy and design mantra behind most ARGs. The game must not openly acknowledge its own fictional status, and all participants should behave as if the events of the game were occurring 'in real life'.

Trout A term coined by a Cloudmaker during The Beast in order to politely point out to newcomers that their comments involved a puzzle which had already been solved, or an idea which had already been considered and followed up by the community previously. Unfiction. com glossary adds: 'Trout is a term of respect that replaces the need to say "you're redundant!" with a courteous term that acknowledges the hard work involved even in redundant efforts.'

Internet Archive (Wayback Machine) The Internet Archive is a non-profit organisation which is building a digital library of internet sites and other cultural artefacts in digital form. In 1996 it began by archiving the internet itself, a medium that was just beginning to grow in use. Content that is otherwise lost in the ephemeral shifts of the web is captured here, which is of specific interest to studies of promotional content, which has a short shelf life. More than 20 years of web history is accessible through the search engine Wayback Machine, which is an invaluable resource for researchers.

Index

Note: numbers in *italics* indicate figures on the corresponding pages.